More Praise for Scott Mason and
Tar Heel Traveler: New Journeys Across North Carolina

"As a native Tar Heel, I am just as avid a fan of Scott Mason and his 'Tar Heel Traveler' as I was about the late Charles Kuralt's 'On the Road.' I hate to miss even one episode. If you ever meet Scott you'll meet a down-home friend."
—Charlie Gaddy, Former WRAL-TV Anchor

If national news makes you sick, then get well with Scott Mason's *Tar Heel Traveler: New Journeys across North Carolina.* And if you like your stuff in a Mason jar, then Scott's the man. He packs entertainment, history, fun, and facts into every story he tells. Thank goodness he keeps those stories alive in books! Treat yourself to a great read for the fireside, the beachside, or the bedside.
—Clyde Edgerton, Author of *Walking Across Egypt and Papadaddy's Book for New Fathers*

By the time Scott Mason wraps up another episode of The Tar Heel Traveler, I feel as though I've taken a trip back home to spend some quality time with an old friend, sipping on a tall glass of sweet tea, sharing a few happy smiles, some easy talk, a smidgen of local news occasionally combined with a bit of toe-tapping' music and some real mouth-watering comfort food. To top it all off, I know I'm always going to come away with a heart brim full of warm and happy memories. That's a mighty fine gift, Scott . . . and I just hope you know how very much all of us appreciate each and every homecoming."
—Ira David Wood III, Executive Director, Theatre in the Park

Scott Mason's engaging delivery and unique knowledge of North Carolina and its roots makes the Tar Heel Traveler the highlight of my evening news. Four nights a week we can count on this charming show to soften the blow of the bad news of the day with delightful stories about people and events "down home." Scott never disappoints.
—Rufus Edmisten, Former Deputy Chief Counsel to Senator Sam J. Ervin's Watergate Committee and Former NC Attorney General and Secretary of State

Scott Mason uses the broad canvas of *The Tarheel Traveler* to paint a portrait filled with detailed images of the people and places that give the state both a unique and universal appeal, a reflection of diversity and individuality, a picture that makes those of us here never want to leave and entices others to come here.
—Bill Thompson, North Carolina Author and Storyteller

TAR HEEL TRAVELER

NEW JOURNEYS ACROSS NORTH CAROLINA

SCOTT MASON

Guilford, Connecticut

Globe
Pequot

An imprint of The Rowman & Littlefield Publishing Group, Inc.
4501 Forbes Blvd., Ste. 200
Lanham, MD 20706
www.rowman.com

Distributed by NATIONAL BOOK NETWORK

British Library Cataloguing in Publication Information available

Library of Congress Cataloging-in-Publication Data available

ISBN 978-1-4930-3751-3 (hardcover)
ISBN 978-1-4930-3752-0 (e-book)

♾™ The paper used in this publication meets the minimum requirements of American National Standard for Information Sciences—Permanence of Paper for Printed Library Materials, ANSI/NISO Z39.48-1992

Printed in the United States of America

TO THE GREAT PEOPLE
OF NORTH CAROLINA, THANK YOU FOR
ALL THE WONDERFUL STORIES.

MANY HAPPY TRAVELS,
AND ENJOY THE ROAD AHEAD!

CONTENTS

LANDMARKS, CURIOSITIES, AND FIRSTS AND THE UNEXPECTED . . .

EPILOGUE

Almost every story has a backstory, usually some funny incident that happened while covering the story. Robert is the photographer I work with, and his favorite story with a backstory is the piece we did on Pantego.

It's a small town—you'll see that term often in the pages ahead; most places we visit are small towns. Pantego really was. Population: fewer than two hundred.

But it did have a school. Or it used to be a school, a historic one built in 1874, that closed a few years before my phone rang with a lady on the line from—"Pantego?" I said.

She laughed and spelled it for me and said it was in Beaufort County, not far from Bath and Belhaven and the pretty Pamlico River. She explained the school had been converted to a museum with the help of a lot of hardworking volunteers. "Oh, it's just beautiful," she said. "And all the history and artifacts we have . . ."

I began to half-listen. Truth is, we don't usually do stories about museums because there's no action. There may be rooms full of interesting items, but they're almost always stiff, stagnant, on display, a visual yawner. I started to yawn, but then she mentioned a rare plaque, and her voice rose. She bubbled over about what they'd uncovered—she and the other tireless volunteers—a plaque of enormous value. They'd found it, rescued it, resuscitated it. "Amazing," she said. "One of a kind. Full of history. Unlike any other. You've got to come see it."

I admit that I was intrigued and not just by what they'd found but by the extent of her enthusiasm. She wasn't a yawner. Plus, I remembered another story nearby we could shoot, one that had lain flat in my file so long it was growing yellow. Two birds with one stone, two stories on one trip. First stop: Pantego.

We drove almost three hours, and when we arrived at that little town of fewer than two hundred, I was surprised it had that many people. There was almost nothing there, just some empty fields and a battered auto garage closed for business.

But there was the old school, a big white building with a red roof, plunked at the end of a barren lot. The building also had a rather interesting architectural doodad: a large, loping archway over the front door. Through the door I marched to see the rare and historic plaque, my mind swirling with something heavy and bronze or shiny and gold.

It was cardboard. Not a plaque at all but a printed piece of paper on cardboard backing. A helpful volunteer explained what was written on it, but I was only half-listening again. I was too stunned. *Surely, this can't be it,* I thought. "This is it?" I said. The woman holding it, the same bubbly one who'd called me, nodded and was even bubblier than before; she pinched the "plaque" at its outermost edges as if scared to leave a smudge mark. Her excitement baffled me. Except this was Pantego, and I supposed there was little else to get excited about.

This wasn't going to work. Robert didn't even bother hoisting the camera on his shoulder; he knew it, too. In desperation, I scoured the room. It wasn't a bad room. The volunteers had turned the old school into a cozy museum and turned the cozy museum into an old school, full of rickety wooden desks, kerosene lamps, and dusty textbooks. "A report card from 1879," said a man, displaying the withered page in his palm. He pointed to a row of 90s in the right-hand column. "A smart one," he announced.

"Yeah, but he got a 72 in Reading," I said, and aimed my finger at the faded pencil mark.

The man took a closer peek. "Well, I imagine that was pretty good in those days."

I wasn't getting anywhere. The new museum, and/or old school, just wasn't enough of a story, no matter the eager volunteers who'd come to welcome us and who moved here and there exclaiming over this and that. I hated to disappoint, and after looking and nodding and trying to smile, I excused myself and wandered outside to clear my head.

I walked a little ways away, away from the bubbling inside, and paced in small circles in the barren lot. There was nothing in the lot, or anywhere in sight, except for the school—a big, clean, crisp, columned, architecturally intriguing, impressive-looking building painted bright white with a roof as red as a fire truck. And a big loping archway over the front door.

I moved closer to inspect then stepped on the porch and took a few more steps until I was only a few feet from the arch and a set of stairs.

The archway was a staircase. Wooden runners rose in a high, steep slope from the porch to a door above the front door. *A door above the door?* But the arch also continued down the other side. I hustled around and, sure enough, there was a second set of stairs identical to its opposite. I stepped back. *Oh, my gosh.* The unusual archway was a double-sided staircase.

Here was my story, my *Aha* moment, a supreme instant of revelation—or elevation. I gazed up at those wonderful, beautiful, magnificent stairs.

When I dashed inside, I must have been bubbling because all the other bubbling abruptly stopped. "The arch," I stammered. "I mean . . . How . . . ? What . . . ? Do you know . . . ?"

A tall, skinny man with a beard as white as the building spoke up; he'd been the least bubbly of the group, one of those laid-back, sleepy-southern-gentleman-farmer types. "Oh, that," he drawled. "Probably the only one of its kind in the world."

I guessed our greeters never considered the staircase a story because they were so used to seeing it. But I don't think they were used to climbing it. The stairs were steep, and so was the age of the friendly volunteers. In fact, some of them had actually graduated from the old Pantego Male and Female Academy. "Two classrooms upstairs," an elderly alumnus told me and explained that kids would scramble up the steps to reach the classroom door above the front door. "Sixth graders used one side, and the other side was for the fifth grade." The man sat for the interview on one of the worn steps; when I'd asked how many stairs there were, he'd walked all the way up and counted all the way down, and now after counting he was panting.

I gathered from the blank faces that nobody had bothered to count the steps before. We found out that day that there were twenty-one on each side of the arch, forty-two total Pantego steps.

Our story on the archway aired a few days later, and the reaction on set was terrific. "The only one of its kind in the world!" the anchorman exclaimed.

"Who would have thought?" the anchorwoman remarked.

Yes, I thought. *Who would have thought? If only they knew . . .*

The "plaque" never even made it into the story.

The *Tar Heel Traveler* debuted on WRAL-TV in Raleigh in 2007. Actually, it first went on the air thirty years before that, but somebody else was the Tar Heel Traveler then, and then somebody else. The series went through myriad changes and then went away altogether, until WRAL dug it up and brought it back. The news director asked me one day if I'd like to quit chasing violent storms and crimes and car wrecks and roam about the state telling warm-hearted features. I thought he was kidding, and then I thought I'd won the lottery. And soon after, my hair turned gray.

Since 2007, Robert and I have shot almost two thousand *Tar Heel Traveler* stories. By the time I'm finished writing this book, we may be looking at three thousand—I'm a slow book writer.

Tar Heel Traveler stories are less than three minutes long, but each one takes about ten hours to shoot, write, and edit. They air four nights a week, Monday through Thursday, at 5:55 p.m. Our audience is large and loyal and would be one viewer bigger if I wasn't so busy writing the next piece. The Tar Heel Traveler rarely gets to see the *Tar Heel Traveler* on the evening news.

But that's okay. I believe I have the best job in all of television. Robert and I have traveled from Murphy to Manteo—and even farther: from Bryson City to Ocracoke Island. We've visited all one hundred North Carolina counties, stayed in luxury hotels, and enjoyed fabulous meals on a company credit card. We've also bunked in roadside motels, eaten out of lunch boxes, and humped from one story to the next, sometimes shooting four or five in a single day. Then I have to write them. My hair is turning grayer by the minute, and the list is growing longer by the mile: nearly two thousand stories and counting . . .

And more than five thousand story ideas. People are constantly emailing me, suggesting good places to visit and great characters to interview. I print out the emails and file them in folders at my desk. Pretty soon I'm going to need a bigger desk.

The work never ends. And neither does the adventure. So many pieces come with surprises: angles I didn't anticipate within the story or incidents that occurred when shooting the story. Almost every story has a backstory.

So many fun stories. So many great memories. So many Bojangles' biscuits and coffee. We've filled up at the pump, and now we're about to fill up again: bacon, egg, and cheese. It's clear sailing once we're through the drive-through. The road waits.

More stories ahead . . .

EARL OWENSBY

THE B-MOVIE LEGEND

I was nervous.

Of course I was. I was headed to a huge movie studio near Charlotte to interview a film legend, a man who had starred in, produced, and directed dozens of classics. Never mind they were B-movie classics.

Earl Owensby had made millions from films many people had never seen. Although somebody must have seen them. CBS's *60 Minutes* once featured a lengthy interview with him, and even Wikipedia had devoted an impressive spread, complete with handsome head shot.

Owensby had a kind of Marlboro Man look, minus the mustache, rugged but dashing. He reminded me of Steve McQueen, whom I'd seen as a kid in *Bullitt,* a movie famous for one long and dramatic car chase. Owensby packed *his* movies with car chases. Plus car crashes, plane crashes, fights, and killings. Low-budget action films were his thing. Big profits were, too.

I had wanted to watch a few of his movies, but they were hard to find, even on the internet, although I had caught a scene or two when the Museum of History in Raleigh highlighted his career. *Hmm,* I thought, gazing at the wide screen on the museum wall. The acting seemed awkward but not terrible, and the production value was decent, the camera angles and editing; I paid attention to that sort of thing.

I had to say, Owensby was fun to watch on film. He had a certain magnetism; it came through in just the few minutes I stood there, arms folded across my chest, eyes on the action. The character he played screeched his car to a stop near a dilapidated barn and climbed out clutching a rifle. I couldn't help but root for him; I liked his look, especially the Stetson on his head. He marched for the door, toward the dark unknown, rifle swinging by his side, and I smiled in anticipation. No doubt about it, the poor sucker inside was gonna get it.

As for me, I did not feel the same bravado as we pulled into Shelby and made our way to Earl Owensby Studios. The on-screen hero was known to chew up bad guys and spit 'em out, and I sure hoped he didn't do that to television reporters in real life.

Robert, on the other hand, was giddy. He knew all about Owensby and his movies, but then he'd been a film major who'd also watched every *Godzilla* remake, even the versions dubbed in Japanese. Robert asked if I'd seen the sci-fi thriller *The Abyss,* which I had in my twenties and enjoyed. "But did Owensby make that?"

Robert told me no, James Cameron had, the same director who later made *Titanic.* For *The Abyss,* Cameron needed a huge space for all the underwater filming. About that time, Earl Owensby had bought an abandoned nuclear power plant in South Carolina with the crazy idea of turning it into a movie set. It suited Cameron fine, and he proceeded to pump seven-and-a-half million gallons of water into the old reactor and shoot several scenes.

I told Robert how ingenious that sounded, though I didn't just mean the movie. I understood *The Abyss* did well at the box office, but I was thinking Owensby did even better with the rent.

When I called to set up my interview, I had left a message on the studio voice mail, which I expected. I'd heard it was an enormous operation, *studios* plural, with buildings as big as warehouses sprawled across two hundred acres in Shelby of all places, a quiet town in the shadow of Charlotte. I figured the film hands were undoubtedly busy and couldn't get to the phone.

But I nearly dropped the phone when Earl Owensby himself called me back a day later. The legend was on the line, and he was friendly and southern, quite country actually, and I wondered if he'd made any westerns. "Was just in Raleigh," he drawled. "At the museum. Nice display they had on me. But sure, you wanna come all this way, you can probably find me."

The *probably* had me worried; I never could pin him down on a time, and even as we neared the complex, I wondered if we'd find him. It occurred to me I was marching toward the unknown myself, just like Earl in the movie clip I'd seen at the museum, but instead of a rifle, all I had was a worn-out notepad. And that's not all that was worn.

A large black sign with crisp white lettering loomed at the top of the drive: "E.O. Studios and Entertainment Center." The sign looked new, but as I'd soon see, nothing else did.

We turned in and rolled down the slope toward a long, low-topped building with windowed doors in the center. The windows were dark, the building dull—whimpering, it seemed, for fresh paint. A separate building sat to the side and was lined with more than a dozen doors. And behind it . . . *Is that a runway?* It was, although I found it hard to picture jetsetters flying in for a splashy stay. The separate building was obviously a motel but with weeds creeping over the stoops.

The whole place had an aura of abandonment. There wasn't a soul in site. Granted, it was a B-movie studio, and Earl Owensby was not Steven Spielberg, but still, I figured there'd be some action even if it had been years since Owensby had shouted, "Action!" He hadn't made a movie in a decade.

Maybe it was the whole sordid, low-budget, B-movie thing or seeing rifle-toting Earl in my mind again stealing into that eerie barn, but I had a slight case of the shivers when I climbed from the car. Movie studio or not, the place was a bit creepy. What else to do but march ahead, except my march was more like a slump-shouldered shuffle toward the tinted double doors.

At least it was bright inside, a small lobby with lots of overhead light. And Earl Owensby larger than life, was there to greet me, here, there, and everywhere, every wall plastered with movie posters, each displaying the chiseled face of the film's steely-eyed hero. The posters were big, slick, and dramatic. I still didn't know about Owensby's acting ability, but he sure looked the part on paper.

Flashy posters would make great video, and I almost told Robert to start shooting. But the polite thing would be to introduce ourselves to the receptionist first. I stuck my head around the corner but saw no sweet lady behind a mahogany desk. I saw nothing, in fact, but a long hallway and didn't hear a sound, either. I could have heard a gun click.

"Hello?" I called, but there was no answer. I told Robert to hang on, I'd check things out, and I began walking down the corridor. I think the movie posters had inspired a bit of the daredevil in me.

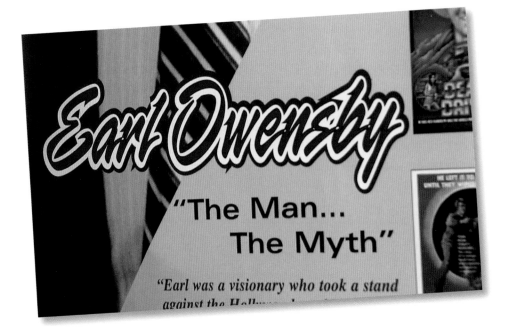

**"The Man...
The Myth"**

"Earl was a visionary who took a stand against the Holl...

There were many open doors and small dark rooms, empty offices apparently, and more posters lining the hallway itself. I walked a few feet before calling "Hello" again, this time without the question mark. We needed to get the show on the road.

It was then I heard a slight ruffle, the riffle of papers maybe, and I eyed door number . . . six? The last door anyway, the one open at the end of the hall.

There at last was the mahogany desk but no sweet lady. Instead, an old gray-haired guy cocked an eye when I entered and slowly rose to his feet. "Hey, there," I said with a wave and toothy grin. "I'm the guy from the television station in Raleigh." The man stepped around the desk, a big fellow indeed, big around, though not especially tall. He wore a short-sleeve black shirt that I guessed was a 2XL. His eyes fixed on mine; his face was tanned but expressionless. I smiled wider. "I'm looking for . . ."

Just as I started speaking, it hit me. I think it was his tan that did it, not a tanning-bed tan but a tough, leathery tan that comes from years of hard work in the hot sun. It was too late to tug back my words. "I'm looking for . . ."—at the last second, I groped for the question mark again. "Earl Owensby?"

"You got him."

There was that voice I'd heard on the phone, but the face from the posters was long gone. And yet it was him: the man, the myth, the legend—I'd seen that very line screaming across one of the posters. He had a presence about him even now, in his early eighties; I'd learned his age from Wikipedia. He stepped with a swagger, and my neck muscles stiffened. I wasn't sure if I'd found the good-guy Earl or the one with both barrels blazing.

"I've heard a lot about you," I said, which was certainly true. It's just that I hadn't *seen* much of him, only about sixty seconds on screen.

"Well, I've made a movie or two," he said, and reached behind him, grabbing a stack of VHS tapes and dumping the pile on his desk. "Yours if you want 'em."

I studied the scattered boxes, especially one with a long-fanged dog on the front, frozen mid-growl or post-bite. The movie's title read *Rottweiler*. Earl must have seen me staring. "I like to call that one Jaws with Paws," he said.

The whole haphazard heap seemed a telling sign. Here was Earl Owensby's story splayed in front of me, his forgotten movies on obsolete tapes. "Grab whatever clips for your story," he said. "Watch 'em if you want—or not. Don't matter."

Actually, I found I did want to watch them. The artwork drew me in, especially a box with that young, lock-jawed, Stetson-clad hero on the cover. Earl had obviously learned how to package himself and his product. Some of his movies had gone on to become cult classics.

Robert thudded in with his gear, wearing a grin, and Earl suddenly seemed energized. Maybe it was catching sight of the television camera. I wondered how long it had been since he'd seen one—or another human being, for that matter. "How about a tour of the place?" he said.

He led us out, and we wound through another long hallway and eventually came to a dining area with tables and booths but with a sepiatone tint, the room lit with one lonely bulb. Earl told me this was where the actors and crew ate. "Good times," he said. I nodded but couldn't quite visualize happy chatter.

The next hall had no bulb. "Dressing rooms," he said with a lazy wave, but I couldn't see much, and I don't think the camera could have, either. Robert hadn't even bothered to power it up yet. No use shooting yellow rooms and dark hallways.

I hoped we were nearing the actual lot where Earl made many of his movies, but he seemed to be taking his time, so I figured I'd egg him on, pump him up. "Quite a place you got here," I said. "You're a legend."

"Well, some say so. But don't believe 'em."

He eventually led us outside, and when my eyes adjusted, I saw we'd come to a long building with a domed roof, the place shaped like an airport hangar. He gave it another one of his lazy waves. This, he said, was one of his studios, and he waved again—*Follow me*—and we slipped past a metal door slid partway open.

It was open enough to allow a wedge of light, and I was surprised at what it revealed: a cavernous space fifty times bigger than my garage. A few blocky movie lights dangled from the ceiling, but otherwise the place was empty except for water puddled on the concrete floor and dried leaves scattered in the corner. "This is huge," I said.

"Got one just like it next door."

In fact, he said he had eight studios on the property, each about fifteen thousand square feet, and I asked just how many movies he'd filmed in Shelby.

"Oh, Lord," said Earl. "At least forty-five. Commercials, too."

I looked around at the enormous space and tried to imagine actors and cameras, but what I couldn't let go of was the puddle. It was big and wide, and I wondered how it got there and if anyone was going to squeegee it up.

"Think this studio will flourish again?" I asked.

Earl looked at me, a trace of a smile on his lips, his big chest thrust out. "I have no doubt," he said slowly, emphatically, so that I couldn't help but give my imagination a second shot. *The man, the myth, the legend.* "But you know," he said, "you do have to have those pictures of Ben Franklin"—his eyes cast a playful twinkle—"the little guy on the hundred-dollar bill."

I found I liked Earl; I liked his directness and dry wit, wrapped in a southern drawl; and maybe some of his directness had rubbed off on me. I told him no need to show us his seven other studios. A sit-down interview instead would be just fine.

We made our way back to the lobby and sat in directors' chairs surrounded by all those movie posters. I started the interview by asking how *he* started, and he took me from the beginning.

He was adopted as a baby, spent his youth in a mill village west of Shelby, and never finished high school, joining the marines instead. After the military, he worked as an industrial supply salesman, and that's when he found his niche and made his money. I wasn't surprised; he seemed to have just the right sales qualities: a country twang that made him instantly likeable but a Rottweiler's bite when it came to Ben Franklins.

He ended up owning five businesses and also enjoyed watching movies. In 1973 he saw *Walking Tall,* a box office hit that earned more than $25 million but cost only half a million to make, and it was all shot in rural Tennessee. Earl figured he could do the same in North Carolina, never mind the fact he knew nothing about making movies. He had never even acted in a high school play.

"I started November 10, 1973." That was the day he began filming his first feature, one called *Challenge*, that he made in Shelby and starred in. He played a good man done wrong, bent on revenge. The catch phrase on the poster read, "They killed his family . . . pushed him to the limit . . . they made a big mistake."

"I went around and hired people that weren't really professional actors, but they could do the part I wanted them to because I was gonna kill 'em off anyway. That's what all our movies are. You ride into town, kill twelve people, and ride out."

Challenge made enough money that Earl began building E.O. Studios on the outskirts of Shelby. Not that the movie was particularly good. One critic compared Earl's acting to a cigar-store Indian; "wooden" was the word he used.

"And then I learned from that one movie there is a foreign market," Earl said, and his eyes widened along with his mouth, revealing a gleaming set of choppers. "I got in the foreign business, and it just started clicking."

He made one movie after another, all following the same formula: action, adventure, death, and destruction. *Dark Sunday, Death Driver, Dogs of Hell.* He acted in some, produced others, generally one film a year, and spent no more than a million dollars on each. That was a formula he stuck with, too, and he raked in the profits.

"Were they good movies?" I asked.

"Well, they sell all over the world, so I'm assuming somebody buys 'em and likes 'em." I noticed he spoke in the present tense, and since he kept flashing his teeth, I figured the profits were still dribbling in.

I asked if he'd mingled with any movie stars, and he searched the ceiling as if trying pluck down a name. "Elvis," he said at last. "Guess he was sorta big."

"Elvis?" I said.

"Nice guy."

"You knew him?"

"Oh, yeah. Named my son Elvis."

"Your son?"

He nodded. "Elvis Owensby."

He told me about playing Elvis in *Living Legend: The King of Rock and Roll.* Earl made the movie in 1980 and costarred with Ginger Alden, who'd been Elvis's fiancé at the time of his death. I watched part of it later and grinned at Earl prancing about the stage, swallowing a microphone. I smiled at his fake sideburns and blue jumpsuit but was taken aback by the voice, which

was amazingly good. I also learned it wasn't his. Earl had lip-synced the songs after hiring a friend to record the soundtrack. The friend was Roy Orbison, a music icon and beloved balladeer.

"Roy Orbison?"

"I used Roy because he was Elvis's favorite singer."

Yet another friend was singer-songwriter David Allen Coe, who in 1977 wrote the country hit *Take This Job and Shove It*. Coe wrote that song while lounging at Earl's swimming pool in Shelby.

Earl was full of surprises. He told me about doing many of his own stunts back in the day, jumping off buildings and driving a car into a house—the house was on fire, of course. He once walked on top of a hot air balloon that floated a mile over the fairgrounds near Shelby. "A mile?" I said. "Weren't you scared?" He shrugged and told me he'd done it to raise money for an orphanage.

I asked if he'd ever dreamed of an Academy Award, which I knew was a silly question. "I don't take it that serious," he said. "Never have."

But he had been serious about profit and had pioneered a trend that helped revolutionize the entire industry. He showed that filmmakers didn't need big-time agents or Hollywood backing or even Hollywood at all. I smiled at a poster on the wall behind him that read, "Once upon a time, Earl Owensby, tool salesman, decided to make movies. Now he wants Hollywood to eat his dust."

Pioneer and *visionary* were words I'd seen reporters use when writing about Earl. And another word often popped up, too: *wives*.

"I been married more than once," he said, speaking out of the side of his mouth. He told me about his eightieth birthday party when all four of his exes happily celebrated with him. "When you have ex-wives show up, something good's happenin'."

I finally thanked him for the interview, and we walked outside, but I kept asking questions. I couldn't help it. Earl was like peeling an onion. I was surprised to learn he'd made a film about Jesus called *The Agony of Christ*.

I looked again at the long white building in need of a whiter coat and at the weedy motel in the distance and the nubby yellow grass—I'd read that Earl mowed it himself. When I first arrived, I had wondered where everybody was. Now I knew there was nobody but us.

He told me he'd fielded many calls from people wanting to borrow his studios to make movies. It's just that none of them had enough of "them little Ben Franklins." Even so, he once again assured me the place would someday flourish. He was convinced, and I wanted to believe him.

"You're famous," I said, hoping to elicit some grand final comment before we left. "All the movies you've made, your success. What's your favorite?"

He looked at the sky as though hoping to see an incoming jet, but there were only clouds. Still, when he turned to me again, his eyes had that playful twinkle. "If you make one and make a profit, that becomes my favorite every time."

Just then, Earl's phone sprang to life, not a normal ring but a loud and familiar melody, and it took me a minute to realize it was the US Marine Corps fight song. I figured some prospective business might be on the line, but Earl merely gazed at the screen and let the tune play, swaying his index finger to the beat as if conducting an orchestra. It was amusing watching him and listening to that stirring rendition, and I thought I might use the moment in my story: Earl, chest out, finger waving. He'd scraped and clawed and chased the American dream and lived the dream on his own terms. I also thought that sounded about as over-the-top as one of his movies—but what the heck.

He waved his finger. And never did answer the phone.

DR. STANLEY

THE SMOKING DOC

The doctor smoked.

He might have been the oldest doctor in the country still practicing medicine. Dr. John Stanley was about to turn ninety-one and still saw patients six days a week.

We pulled into Woodland, a town of about seven hundred in rural Northampton County. Our navigation system took us right to the building—although I wasn't so sure. I peered out the car window at a place on the corner that looked like a small olive-colored house, desperate for a new coat of olive. Shutters on the window and twin benches in front attempted to add a homey touch, although the splintered slats on one bench hung

loosely beneath the seat. I didn't see a sign or anything to indicate a doctor's office. I didn't even see any people; the street was lonely. I checked the address again and shrugged, and we rolled into a gravel lot beside the building and parked.

Now I did see a sign, and how odd. A stop sign jutted from the wall, and it was utterly washed out, not a trace of red, just grayish-white. And why a stop sign facing a parking lot anyway? It was so peculiar, I asked Robert to shoot it, thinking maybe I could use it in the story—if we had a story. I wasn't even sure we had the right place.

I walked around the corner to the front, still searching for a "Dr. John Stanley" plaque, and when I reached the door, I debated whether to knock. I tapped twice, waited a beat, and pushed it open.

I hadn't known what to expect, but I certainly didn't expect a wallop in the face. It hit me as soon as I entered, overwhelmed me, in fact: the bitter smell of cigarette smoke. Camels, I bet. The place reeked, air so thick I gasped then coughed but muffled it with my arm because of the lady at the desk a few feet ahead. She was smiling behind the windowless half-wall, hands folded in front of her as though she'd been expecting me. I gathered myself as quickly as I could for I was pretty sure I *was* in the right place. I noticed dog-eared magazines piled on a table, but the real give-away was the woman herself, clad in one of those white doctor jackets. It was everything I could do to return her smile while keeping my eyes from leaking.

As a reporter, I can never be sure what I'll find when I walk into a story, no matter the calls I've made and research I've done. Nothing is ever 100 percent. Indeed, this story had seemed fifty/fifty. I'd spoken to the doctor on the phone and felt sure of his mind, but his voice sounded as ancient as he was. It was as raspy as sandpaper. No wonder.

My clouded mind swam as I wobbled toward the woman. I had all kinds of doubts and yet felt oddly inspired, too. *A ninety-year-old doctor? Smoke-filled office? Washed-out stop sign?* My would-be story was piling up with "dog-eared" angles, which was actually a good thing; I treasure pieces that aren't predictable. My throat burned, but my heart fluttered. I had the feeling I was onto something—though at that point, I needed to grab something.

I reached for the half-wall and croaked out my name. "Of course you are," she said—*her* voice was raspy, too. She said she watched me on television and told me she was Dr. Stanley's daughter; she had to be pushing seventy. "I'll get him up from his nap," she said, and rose from her chair just as Robert clanged in with the camera.

"Wait a minute," I barked. She'd already turned for the hall. "Can I clip a little microphone to you?" She shrugged, and I fumbled the cord under her jacket, and down the hall she went, stopping at the last door on the right. She pushed it open ever so gently and crept in.

"Daddy? Daddy?" she whispered. The camera transmitted her voice, though the lens was trained on nothing but the long hall and dark doorway at the end. "Daddy, the guy is here to speak with you."

I saw it all in my head—and Alfred Hitchcock popped into mind, too. The old filmmaker was known to direct a scene in which the action off camera was sometimes more powerful than on. The "pictures" were better.

"Huh? He's here?" Another voice, the one I'd heard on the phone. The camera grumbled with lots of grunting and stirring, and finally his daughter appeared and said he'd be right with us. We all waited, staring at the empty hall, anticipation rising, tension at its Alfred Hitchcock highest.

At last came Dr. Stanley, the man I'd heard so much about, who so many people apparently knew and trusted, quite likely the oldest working doctor in all of America. His bed-head hair looked like it had been caught in a dentist's drill. His blue suit was wrinkled, red tie askew, whiskered face drawn, and eyes bleary. He used the wall like a crutch and hobbled ahead, one shaky step at a time. We caught his appearance on camera—and I wondered if we should have.

He shuffled past us, entered an open room, and fell into a ratty chair in the corner. The chair fit the décor. Dr. Stanley's office was cluttered with papers piled everywhere. One stack teetered two feet high, and I worried about shaking the floor. His bulletin board was a mishmash of pictures curled at the edges, hanging cockeyed by colored thumbtacks. The wall phone was caddywhompus, too, requiring a hard lean sideways to see the numbers. Yellow sticky notes clung to the phone, the wall, the lamp, adding more confetti to the mess.

I tried a warm smile and politely asked if he wouldn't mind sitting in his desk chair, the one in the middle of the room. I said it would be better for the interview rather than being backed into the corner. The question landed heavier than Dr. Stanley had. He wasn't going anywhere; I'm not sure he could have without significantly more grunting. "That's where he always sits," piped his daughter, leaning her head in. "His favorite chair."

His favorite chair it was. I took the desk chair. "Well . . . ," I began, slapping my hands on my thighs. "How old are you?" I said much too loudly, assuming hearing aids. What I saw instead was a cigarette.

He plucked one from a pack buried beneath yesterday's newspaper and dangled it between two fingers. "Ninety," he said, his thin lips tight.

I almost forgot what I'd asked him. My mind had grown foggy again, and he hadn't even lit up. There was suddenly an elephant in the room—and maybe a Camel, too—thin and white but one that weighed a ton. The pause was so heavy I felt my throat tighten and groped for my voice. "What year did you go to med school?" Best to ignore the elephant, I thought.

"Nineteen fifty."

"When did you start practicing?"

"Fifty-five."

I was going for the basics, and that's what he was giving me in return, although one- and two-word answers weren't enough. I needed more. But at least I had time.

On the doctor's advice, I'd scheduled the story for early afternoon. He'd told me on the phone the office closed for lunch and said that would be the best time for the interview because he might be busy afterward—though I doubted that now. *Busy? Here?* I asked why he picked Northampton County and Woodland of all places.

"Woodland was *boooooming*," he said. "Had industry all around."

I'd apparently struck a nerve; he reacted at last and told me he'd grown up in South Carolina and had stumbled upon Woodland by accident, just passing through, but that he'd taken a moment to look around and was impressed.

"I thought it would be the best place," he said. "First patient I had, a man drove up with his mule and said, 'I want you to treat my mule, and if you do good, then I'll come see you myself.'"

My mind wasn't foggy anymore. "What happened? Did you treat the mule?"

"Oh, yeah."

"And did the man come see you?"

"Yup."

The doctor had struck *my* nerve; he'd tapped my funny bone, and I laughed. And then he sucked the wind out of me.

He drew the cigarette to his lips and fired up his Bic for all to see, including the camera. I watched the flame climb and thought about jumping in to stop him, warning him that smoking on television could ruin his career. But then again, he *was* ninety. Plus, I had a feeling this was simply who he was, that a cigarette for him was like an ink pen to most doctors; it was his "signature."

"How long have you smoked?" I figured his lighting up gave me permission to ask.

"Since I was in the Boy Scouts." He spoke with a southern bent and drew out *Boy Scouts*, tapping my funny bone again, but I quickly shook off the grin and narrowed my eyes.

"Some people might say, 'A doctor smoking? Oh, my gosh!' How would you respond to that?"

"It's just too bad a habit and strong."

He drew a long puff—the nail on his index finger was yellow—and blew a cloud of smoke.

"Have you ever tried to stop?"

"I've tried several times, but it doesn't last long."

I think I knew, sitting in that cluttered office, watching Dr. Stanley puff on his cigarette on camera with no apparent shame at all, that this might actually make him the most popular doctor in America, not to mention the oldest, for the public often admires a flawed character, one who's vulnerable, the underdog—or under-doc. He said he believed smoking had even made him a better doctor because it helped calm his nerves, and he told me about the lives he'd saved and babies he'd delivered.

"I was averaging one baby a day." He said that during Woodland's heyday, he often delivered them at homes instead of in a hospital. He told me he'd delivered several thousand babies during his career. "And twenty-two in one weekend."

"Twenty-two?"

Turned out, every doctor from counties around had been off at a convention. "Twenty-two," he said, and drew another puff, and I let the silence hang, and the smoke, too, allowing him and the camera both to savor the moment.

"My biggest trouble now is the numb hands and feet from the chemo."

I had known about the cancer and was about to bring it up when he did instead. "Had two cancers. Ignored all the signs and symptoms for three-and-a-half years. Crazy," he said, and sized up the cigarette between his fingers. It had gone out, and he raised it to his lips and held up his lighter. "We think we can't get sick," he said and flicked, and the flame jumped.

He blew out a smoky breath and said his prognosis was good, that he felt fine and had a new lease on life. He allowed himself a smile and told me about his woodworking hobby. "I built my own coffin," he said, and offered to show it to me later at home. He kept the coffin in his living room and admitted he was proud of it—but happy it was empty.

I began to hear noise coming from the lobby, people talking, and hoped a patient had walked in; we would need video of the doctor examining someone. I recognized one of the muffled voices as the doctor's daughter. "My little angel," he said when I asked about her. He said he had a younger daughter, too, and a wife of more than sixty years. "Married in fifty-two," he said, and his eyes puddled, though not from the smoke. She had been gone two years now. "I still miss her badly."

The noise in the back grew louder, and I checked my watch. It was 2:00 p.m. and office hours again, and soon his daughter poked her head in and said he was needed. "Patients?" I asked, and she nodded and pointed up and down the hall then bent to help her dad up once he'd snuffed his cigarette.

He walked stiff-legged across the corridor, and, frankly, so did I; we'd both been sitting a while. A middle-aged woman waited in a room and told him the camera was welcome, too, then proceeded to explain her ailments. She said she hadn't been feeling well, and Dr. Stanley did all the normal doctor things: felt her throat, listened to her heart, peeked in her ears. "Say 'Ahhhh.'" I figured he'd tell her to take a couple of aspirin and call him in the morning, but after a few more questions and a bit more poking, he diagnosed the problem. "It's your sinuses. Backed up in there." He scribbled on a pad, tore off the sheet, and handed it to her. The woman accepted it with both hands—that little paper like a bar of gold—and thanked the doctor profusely, although he was very businesslike, merely nodding as he rose and crossed the hall to another room and another patient.

This one was a young black man, a truck driver with a nagging back who didn't hesitate pulling up his shirt and letting the doctor jab. The man described the lingering strain, and yet his face actually brightened during the thump-thumps, even more when Dr. Stanley told him how to treat it. The truck driver looked like he felt better already.

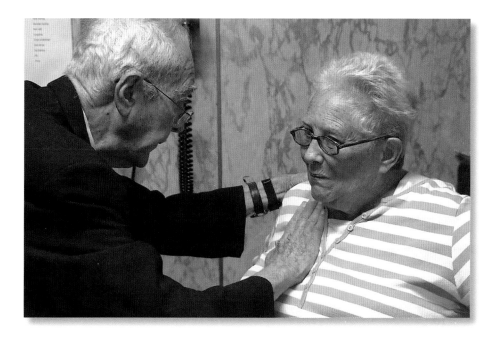

Dr. Stanley treated all kinds: young, old, black, white, truckers, house-wives. Didn't matter. Every face seemed to brighten when he walked in—although I suppose the patients could've been tickled by his bed hair.

There weren't enough rooms. They were all occupied, and so was the lobby. "Some days we see two people, some days twenty," said his daughter, holding the door open for a stout woman with a walker. She gripped the handles and humped it over the threshold, banging the aluminum legs, while panting and wincing. "My ribs."

Her voice was so whispery and desperate, her face so painfully pinched, that I jumped in to help. I grabbed the door, allowing Dr. Stanley's daughter to help the poor woman into the lobby. Then the daughter threw me a look that said *Stick to her like stitches,* and off she went to check on a room.

I was left with the walker woman, along with an awkward silence—well, except for the panting. "I fell," she finally whispered between gasps. "My ribs."

"Oh, I know how you feel," I said, though I wasn't sure I did, but I tried my best to comfort her. I told her about playing hockey a few years back and slamming into the boards. "Just bruised them," I said, "but they took forever to heal." *Uh oh*, I thought and could have kicked myself—though preferably not in the ribs. I should have omitted "forever."

"What if they're broke?" She peered up at me, and her weepy eyes made me think they might be.

"I don't know," I said and shrugged. "With ribs, I think you have to let 'em heal on their own." I could have kicked myself again; that sounded like forever, too. "But you'll be okay," I quickly added. "Dr. Stanley will know what to do." I offered the warmest smile I could. Indeed, after interviewing Dr. Stanley and watching him work, I felt he *would* know what to do. "You been coming here long?"

"Oh, I been knowing him forty-five, fifty years." She was only half-panting now and told me she'd walked to the office from her home a half mile away.

Now I was the one gasping for breath. "What? In your condition?" I shook my head. "Must be a good doctor."

"God, yes," she said, and a grin spread over the grimace. "He's the best."

The doctor's daughter returned, and together she and the walker woman humped down the hall and rattled into an end room. Dr. Stanley was gentle, pressing a flat hand to her chest and side. "Does that hurt? How about here?"

"Yes, yes," she whispered through clenched teeth. "Hurts so bad." I grimaced myself just watching her.

He asked questions, made notes, and rather surprisingly said he didn't think the ribs were broken. *Good news*, I thought, though he did prescribe an X-ray just to make sure. I figured either way she was in for a long recovery—though I worried more about her long walk home. I felt better when I saw somebody pull up to give her a ride.

The doctor had other patients to see, and while he tended to them, I admired the walls, the yellowed diplomas, and family snapshots; he had lots of grandchildren. I noticed a couple of Norman Rockwell paintings, one of a frightened wide-eyed boy with his britches halfway down while the doctor prepared a long needle. But I thought the more fitting Rockwell print was one of a kindly physician—with bed hair, too, as a matter of fact—his stethoscope placed over a doll's heart to the great satisfaction of the freckly girl clutching her raggedy companion.

When he wasn't seeing patients, Dr. Stanley was in his crowded office, in his corner chair, cigarette in hand, hunched over paperwork, although I realized it wasn't medical work but a crossword puzzle. "I do three or four a day," he said. I leaned over him, curious to see how he was doing. He'd filled almost every blank, down and across. "I do them in ink."

Ups and downs . . . I'm sure the doctor had experienced many in his ninety years: the people he'd saved and those he couldn't; the death of his wife and his own close call with cancer; the loyalty of his patients and relationship with his daughter. Geneva was her name. "A wonderful boss," she'd told me earlier and pointed to a framed needlepoint sign near her desk. It read "M.D. Means My Daddy."

Dr. Stanley inked in the final squares of his puzzle and drew a long puff. "Do your patients ever say, 'Doctor, you need to quit smoking?'" I didn't want to belabor the point but knew every viewer watching the story would probably be asking the same question.

"Oh, many times," he said.

I also knew every viewer would probably be glued to the screen, for when Dr. Stanley spoke, the tobacco he had breathed in billowed out, and his smoke-filled face and matter-of-fact manner made for unpredictable television. Plus, his timing was impeccable. "I tell 'em I'm just too old to know better," he said with the smoke at its smokiest.

I thanked him for his time, thanked him rather profusely myself, and hugged his daughter and even some of the patients. They were all so friendly and nice. No wonder the office looked like a home. Norman Rockwell would have loved this place, I thought, stepping outside and turning back for a last look at the olive-green building. Not a doctor sign in sight, and yet people had found their way.

What I did notice, what I hadn't seen before, were three funny figures in the window, propped on the inside sill, little plastic bobble-headed toys: a nodding pig, Hawaiian belly dancer, and grinning owl with oversized eyes even for an owl. I told Robert to shoot each one. Like the faded stop sign I'd seen earlier, somehow I knew I'd write to them.

In the story that eventually aired, Dr. Stanley said he was too old to know better, and the pig nodded. He said his cancer prognosis was good, and the Hawaiian girl danced. I told viewers he was still seeing patients, and the grinning owl peered.

"You going to keep practicing?" I had asked him at the end of the interview.

"Long as I can," he said, and smiled behind the smoke, though I could see his smile quite clearly.

The doctor is in, I said in my story. *Six days a week, with no plans to STOP.*

MONIQUE JOHNSON

TWO FEET OF INSPIRATION

She is twenty-four inches tall.

"Just two feet?"

"Just two feet. A *powerful* two feet," she said and jabbed her hand at me to emphasize the point. "But just two feet."

Monique Johnson was born with a rare type of dwarfism. Two feet tall isn't much higher than people's knees. She did have the advantage of sitting in a wheelchair, so she could at least talk to someone at eye level when seated at a table. "Doctors are astonished I'm even still alive," she told me. They hadn't expected her to live past six years old; her spine was so curved they thought she might squash her lungs.

When I spoke to her, she was twenty-eight and smiling and poking her hand at me. Her hand was less than half the size of mine, and she gestured with her whole hand rather than stabbing an index finger at the air to make a point. She couldn't close her fingers because they were too short, and so she had no way to make a pointed one that would stand out. And yet Monique stood out. "I've had a pretty normal life," she said.

"Normal?" I asked.

She shrugged like it was no big deal.

"But just twenty-four inches tall?" I said, pressing her a bit, not entirely convinced by her nonchalant shrug. I was thinking instead of obstacles and hardships, not to mention prejudice. Monique was also a minority; she was black.

She shrugged again. "I just take any lemons and make lemonade."

I suppose she had led a fairly "normal" life. She grew up in Winston-Salem, had plenty of friends, and went to public high school. She navigated the hallways in her wheelchair. During her senior year, she signed up for an elective, an entry-level art class, and that's when she discovered, quite by accident, that she had an artistic gift. It wasn't long before her classmates were in for a discovery, too.

"No one had ever seen me walk before," Monique told me. She used a wheelchair because she was born with clubfeet, which made it painful to stand. But for high school graduation, she was determined to walk across the stage. And so she did.

I watched home video of the ceremony, and it was such a stirring moment. Out she comes in cap and gown, no hesitation at all, and the whole place erupts. People are cheering and shouting as she totters across the stage, walking surprisingly fast. In fact, she moves so quickly the dignitaries seated on stage are slow getting to their feet, even though it sounds like everybody else already is; it sounds like a standing ovation.

The row of men in suits and ties are only halfway out of their chairs when Monique passes, and they're trying to applaud even though it's awkward. It's as if it has dawned on them, finally, that this is *the* moment of the whole graduation. Monique doesn't slow down.

She reaches the man at the end of the line, who squats like a baseball catcher to hand her the diploma, although he actually loses his balance and sticks two fingers to the floor to steady himself. The applause doesn't let up, and for good reason. I had learned Monique's grade point average was 4.0. She graduated at the top of her class—at twenty-four inches tall.

She graduated twice more, from college at North Carolina A&T State University and from law school at Elon University. I found a picture of her online that showed her at a table, pouring over papers next to her laptop. She looked like any other student at the law library, very intense. She looked like she'd be a good lawyer, although she once told a reporter she wanted to be a judge.

Reporters were often intrigued by her story, and the articles they printed piqued other people's interest. Soon, she was accepting invitations to speak and found she had a knack for inspiring others. Sometimes she used her art as an added wow factor. Audiences would be transfixed when she unveiled paintings six feet tall, three times her size. Her art and ability to inspire were shifting her away from a career in law. She found she was becoming a voice for people with disabilities. Art and motivational speaking, she believed, were the paths God had set for her.

I visualized my story before I called her. I would interview Monique in her art studio, paintbrush in hand, surrounded by all her colorful work. I had seen her art; she tended to paint dazzling abstracts with lots of swirly blues, purples, and yellows. I pictured her telling me about her life and inspirational journey while creating yet another striking original.

She sounded on the phone the way she looked on my computer: Pleasant but busy. The online images usually showed her painting or speaking. She traveled a great deal, giving speeches all over the country, and filled me in on her upcoming schedule, while I briefed her on mine. Turned out, there was only one possible day we had in common anytime soon. "That works," I said. "We'll come to your studio."

"Actually, I'm speaking at a conference that day. It's in Greensboro, but it's *all* day."

I think she must have heard my heavy sigh through the phone line.

"But I can probably break for a little while," she said. "You could interview me out back. I think there's a picnic area near the parking lot."

I heard *picnic area* and *parking lot* and cringed and explained it wasn't just an interview I needed but video of her actually painting. Plus, as many of her finished pieces as she had. I told her it would be a great story, that she was a real inspiration, and I was hoping she'd say okay and skip the conference altogether.

"I can paint on the picnic table," she said. "I'll bring my palette and some of my art."

I rubbed my forehead and thought about giving up, telling her no, that I'd call her again later when she had more time. But I remembered waiting for other stories to develop in the past that never did and didn't want to risk the same with Monique. I knew she did have a great story; I could tell by the articles I had read and pictures I'd seen—and by the voice on the phone. The voice had a certain "Manhattan" to it. That's where she had lived until about age four, and I could hear a little swagger. She sounded

part New York, part North Carolina, edgy but hospitable. She didn't sound little but rather like someone big and confident. It was me who sounded small. "Well . . . ," I said, still hoping she'd scrap the conference but knowing she wouldn't. "I guess we can make that work."

But I had my doubts.

It was just as I'd imagined: asphalt lot, brick building, and a small grassy area with iron outdoor furniture, the kind with decorative curly cues. The picnic table looked like it weighed a ton—and probably did so no one would steal it. There was barely a tree in sight or whiff of air. I didn't even hear birds chirp; I think the building was so blocky it muffled any sound.

We'd parked behind the building, and I made my way to the back door, making sure to keep to the walkway for fear the grass might be under surveillance. Step on a blade and I could be zapped. Admittedly, I was both cynical and skeptical walking in.

I didn't know what I'd find inside. Of course, I hoped I'd find Monique, but even then, I wasn't sure what I'd find. I had never laid eyes on a two-foot-tall person. It was tough to picture, even though I'd seen her picture.

She wasn't in the lobby, at least I didn't think so. But there was a young African-American woman whose eyes met mine. "You with the TV?" she said in a soft voice.

She introduced herself as Monique's younger sister, which I found surprising given her seemingly shy nature and five-foot-something stature. "I'll be right back," she said and slipped into the auditorium.

A moment later, she walked out with Monique rolling by her side in her wheelchair, the electric kind with a joystick. I had to bend to shake her hand, and when I did I thought of the crouching man at her high school graduation. I hated to be looking down, didn't want to appear demeaning or patronizing, but squatting like a baseball catcher might have been worse. I don't think Monique gave it a thought either way. "Let's go outside," she said.

She pulled up to the iron table, while her sister collected Monique's palette and paintings from the car. The paintings were on poster boards, which her sister propped on easels; they'd brought some of those, too. It was certainly not the ideal setup, this semicircle display in back of the building, but what choice did I have?

Monique squeezed several tubes, blotting paint onto her palette, and then began mixing and dabbing and finally painting. I think she knew we needed the video, and Robert tried to capture her from every angle, even shooting through the iron curly cues—I think *he* knew the story needed some oomph.

I let Robert shoot and Monique paint, which allowed me time to check

out her work. I looked at one piece where she'd highlighted several musical instruments, including a curvy keyboard painted as though it was floating amid waves of purple, orange, and red. Another piece showed the bluish outline of a translucent man tooting a trumpet, and still another was of a colorful bird with its wings outstretched and a single word scrolled at the bottom: *Believe*.

"When people see my art, they first appreciate the work. But their eyes light up when they see the artist."

She wore pearl earrings and a red-checked sleeveless shirt and rested her arms on her wheelchair. "I decided to live each and every day to the fullest." Her face was somewhat long, and when she smiled, a dimple appeared on her left cheek. "You know, I would say life is a blank canvas. You're fully equipped with what you have or what you need to succeed."

It was a nice thought, but I had also been watching her paint and knew it couldn't be easy, because she *wasn't* fully equipped. And so I risked my next question, hoping it wouldn't offend. "Is it hard physically for you to paint and grip the paintbrush?"

"Oh, it is, because my fingers don't close. So you're looking at gripping anything just like this." She demonstrated by balancing the brush between the tips of two fingers. "Threading it through them," she said. I nodded but knew the hard part would be keeping the brush in place when she pressed it to the canvas; there wouldn't be any leverage to stop it from slipping. And yet once again, Monique demonstrated her ability to overcome the odds.

She dipped the brush in the paint and went to work on the canvas. She painted mainly with a back-and-forth motion, as if scribbling with a pencil, but it worked.

"What can't you do?" I asked. "Do you go to restaurants, movies?"

"Oh, absolutely," she said and set the brush down and rested her sleeveless arms on the wheelchair again, and I was struck by how supremely confident she looked, like a woman in a muscle shirt who isn't afraid of anything.

"Do people stare?" I asked. "Does it bother you?"

"Oh sure, they stare. You know, I might hear a young person say, 'Mom, is that a baby?' You know, they're wondering, *Does she have legs?* I grab their attention because they don't know, and I love people at that point. At that point, I can shine."

What I think she meant was that she could teach, could upset whatever preconceived notions people might have about a two-foot-tall woman in a wheelchair. I think she was grateful for the chance to make people . . . *Believe.*

I admired all her work, but my favorite was one she'd painted of a tree. Its gangly branches were crooked and bare, but from behind the tree came streaks of red and gold, like rays of light radiating out, filling not just the space between the limbs but the entire canvas, leaving no white space at all. The tree didn't need leaves. The colors made it powerful and statuesque, its arthritic limbs striking and beautiful.

I realized then that it made no difference where I had interviewed Monique. Her home studio would have been nice, but her story superseded the setting; it was that compelling.

She had reminded me that the story is the thing, that it wasn't the frills that mattered. In this case, what mattered was Monique, front and center, all twenty-four inches of her. She was both inspiring and entertaining. And also funny. I hadn't expected her to have a sense of humor, but Monique had upset my preconceived notions, too.

"Are you angry?" I asked. "Bitter?"

"No, not at all." She shook her head as if to add, *Definitely not!* "If I could make the wish that I could be five-and-a-half feet tall for just a week, of course. Why not experience it? But after that, I would have to go back to my two-foot sassy way of just living life and enjoying life and making an impact."

I might have found that hard to believe before I met her, that she didn't want to be . . . *normal*. I wondered if she might paint that word one day, floating across the canvas. But I believed Monique now. She was the kind of person who meant what she said.

"Why fit in if you can stand out?" She shrugged and smiled, and the dimple formed on her cheek again.

I smiled back. It was hard not to.

MARY AND MILDRED

IDENTICAL TWINS

I did a double take and nearly ran into the door.

Robert was holding it open, and I turned to see it just in time. We were walking into a restaurant in Wilson with Keith leading the way. He was a photographer for the local paper who'd become a friend and good source of info. He often sent me story ideas—and then I learned he was a story himself. He'd been taking pictures of old tobacco barns, documenting those dilapidated relics before they disappeared, and planned to publish a book, the coffee-table type with glossy spreads of the sagging structures.

We had tromped through fields that morning, Robert shooting him shooting the barns, while I nosed around and watched for snakes. I interviewed Keith and soon had myself another story with another one to get to in twenty minutes and one after that as well. Except my phone buzzed just as I'd safely settled in the car, snake-bite free and pants in one piece. I was sure a rusty nail from a loose board would have snagged my pocket and shredded my khakis, but I was good. And then I was bad.

The caller was canceling. It was my next story, and something had come up. "Sorry," he said. "How about next week?"

Maybe it was a blessing in disguise. We could eat lunch, and how often did we do that? Almost never. And to be in Wilson, land of so many great mom-and-pop classics . . . We couldn't have asked for a better spot. Robert and I had two hours until our afternoon shoot. We told Keith to pick the place. We'd treat.

He chose the Creamery, a longtime landmark, and I could hear my stomach growling while we were walking across the parking lot. Keith and Robert's might have been growling more, because they'd scurried on ahead of me. But at least Robert had politely stopped to hold open the restaurant door. I assumed he was holding it open for me, but it could have been for the two elderly ladies walking out of the Creamery just as I was about to walk in. We passed, and I smiled, but they were chatting, and I don't think they noticed. Mine was a routine smile, an absent-minded glance—my thoughts were on fried chicken and mashed potatoes—and I turned my eyes to the door again. But in the next second that followed, my subconscious kicked in, the chicken flew away, and I swung my head around to take another look at them.

The ladies wore identical outfits—white blouses and long blue skirts—and I swear, their faces had been identical, too, even down to their eyeglasses, although I had just caught a glimpse. By this time they were well past me—with the door right in front of me.

I whipped my head back around. My khakis had survived the splintered barns, but the door frame threatened to crunch my nose. I pivoted just in time.

Once inside, I stood with Robert and Keith at the counter, reading the overhead menu, waiting to place my order. Except I wasn't really reading or waiting. I was thinking of those ladies and their look-alike faces and identical outfits. I was thinking they were a story.

My mind kept telling me one thing, my belly another. Story or fried chicken? I felt like a wishbone pulled in two different directions. The pull of those ladies was stronger. I held up my finger. "I'll be right back," I told Robert and Keith and dashed out the door.

The women weren't in the parking lot as far as I could tell. I looked left and right—nothing. But then I checked the cars, and—there! I spotted

two gray heads through the rear window of an old blue clunker, idling in a corner space. I ran up, tapped a knuckle on the door, smiled, and waved my notepad. I don't write many notes in my notepad, but it can be a handy prop. I think the lady behind the wheel thought I was a policeman. She smiled back and began rolling down her window—it was the old hand-crank kind.

"Hello," I said. "Sorry to bother you, but, I mean, well, you're not gonna believe this, but I'm a television reporter from Raleigh, and you two just look like a story."

The wishbone again. The lady was either going to crank the window up or keep smiling. Turned out, it was my lucky day.

"Yes," she said. "Identical twins." The two of them giggled and then began talking at the same time, and I really didn't have to say anything else. Or think anything else. I just knew, standing there, hearing them, seeing them, that I had a story.

"Can I interview you?" I finally interrupted. "Could a photographer and I come to your house, say, in half an hour?"

I could hardly believe what I was asking, especially with two leisurely hours ahead of me and famous fried chicken behind me. But of course I figured they'd say no, certainly not. Invite some strangers over?

"Sure," they giggled and gave me their names: Mary and Mildred. They told me they lived two doors from each other but agreed on Mary's place for the interview. "Half hour will be fine," they said.

I walked back in the Creamery in a daze, not quite believing the opportunity that had landed in my lap. And not quite tasting the fried chicken heaped on my plate. I'm sure it was good. But the promise of a good story was even better.

Keith went on his way after lunch, and so Robert and I pulled up to the little brick apartment where Mary and Mildred were waiting. "The Elliott sisters," they said, formally introducing themselves but greeting us like old friends. They even offered pie and coffee.

They sat together on the couch, smiling and chatting, and I kept glancing from one to the other. They looked and even sounded alike, but I could tell a difference. Mary was slightly smaller, Mildred slightly quieter, but they complemented each other—even when they didn't.

"She will not make a decision," Mary said. "I have to make the decision."

"She's five minutes older than I am," Mildred said. "She's the boss."

They laughed and patted the laps of their blue skirts. "I never pay any attention to what she has on," Mary said, "and nine times out of ten, I've got on the same thing she has."

They told me they had dressed alike even as little girls growing up in Wilson.

"Always dressed like little dolls," Mildred said. "You talk about a time we had."

They pulled out photos dating back to when they were toddlers, then in their teens and twenties. "A time we had," Mary said, echoing Mildred, and I glanced up to see them smiling, then continued thumbing through the stack.

I saw them pictured with their husbands, old black-and-white eight by tens. "Married brothers," Mildred said, and I did my second double take. Even their husbands looked alike.

"You married *brothers*?"

"They walked into the church and spied us," Mary said, and that was the beginning. Mary married Luther Elliott, and Mildred married Marvin Elliott. The Elliott brothers weren't twins, but they might as well have been. "We had a wonderful relationship as couples, we really did," Mary said.

"We surely did," Mildred said.

"I always said my marriage was from heaven," Mary added, and Mildred nodded.

"He told me that morning he felt bad," Mildred said, and now Mary nodded. The sisters had lost their husbands at nearly the same time.

"Two months and six days after her husband died," Mary said.

"And they'd both worked at the same place," Mildred said.

Mary and Mildred also talked about the loss of their sister—it hadn't occurred to me they had another sister. "She would come every night," Mary said, "and we'd all three go out to dinner."

"Every night," Mildred said.

"Every night," Mary added. "But we've had to accept that she's gone, because that's life." They both nodded.

I asked Mary and Mildred if they ever argued.

"Somewhat."

"Somewhat."

"But it doesn't amount to anything."

"Doesn't amount to anything."

They patted their laps and told me they were eighty-five years old and saw each other every day.

"Sometimes when she comes in, I've got a good hot meal," Mary said.

"That's right," Mildred said.

"That's right," Mary said.

I'm not sure I could have planned a better story, not even if I'd had months, or even years, to scour the state. It was like fate had led me to them. Or luck. A double take is what it took.

I asked them for any final thoughts, knowing I still had another story to get to, and what they said came as yet another surprise, for they spoke, not as one but as two. They were twins but also individuals, they said—which was less surprising the more I thought about it. They did have different personalities: Mary chatty, Mildred shy, and they lived separately, though only two doors apart, when they could just as easily have lived together. Instead, they had fashioned their own lives, created their own memories, established their own independence. They were identical but with their own identities.

"That's one thing you learn through life," Mary said. "You can't always depend on others. You have to learn to do it yourself."

"Do it yourself," Mildred said, and they both nodded and patted their laps.

***

Mildred was ninety-one when she died in 2016, Mary ninety-three when she passed in 2018. I heard they'd been thrilled with our story—and each time we reran the story. And because of the story, the Elliott sisters became Wilson celebrities, or something akin to that—the identical twins from television.

I think about them sometimes when straining over another script, worrying over the next line. Will it matter what words I choose? Will anybody notice? Will the story make a difference? Then I remember Mary and Mildred, whose story lives on like an enduring echo, even now, years after their deaths. Viewers tell me they remember the Elliott sisters, and they smile when they tell me.

Those smiles are like enduring echoes, too.

PERCY FLOWERS AND THE GROCERY BAG

MOONSHINE AND HOT DOGS

The almost-famous hot dog is famous.

And so is the name on the store that sells them: the Percy Flowers Store in Clayton.

Percy Flowers, the man, was not only famous but infamous. All these years later, people in North Carolina still talk about him, which could be a case of the myth outgrowing the man. Percy seemed like a simple man. He'd been one of nine children who left school after seventh grade to work on the farm in rural Johnston County. The farm later became his. He grew tobacco and cotton and also ran a country store.

He was apparently a good businessman—and maybe not so simple after all. Even in old photos, the hard stare behind his round glasses makes him look like he's thinking—perhaps thinking ahead. Trying to stay a step ahead of the law.

King of the Moonshiners, declared the *Saturday Evening Post,* which blared that headline across its August 2, 1958, issue. The popular *Post* informed readers across the country that Percy Flowers was one of the greatest moonshiners who ever set foot on God's great swath of southern soil. According to the *Post,* he produced illegal liquor on five thousand acres, which supposedly earned him a million dollars a year tax-free. But rather than keep all that money, he lavished much of it on his church and helped others in need. He might have been the South's greatest philanthropist, too, a Robin Hood–like folk hero with a loving wife and two kids—and possibly some illegitimate kids.

Between 1929 and 1958, grand juries indicted Percy twenty-eight times on charges ranging from bootlegging to tax evasion, but he spent only about a year in jail. The law had a hard time touching him or tainting his reputation. Even the judge who sentenced him pointed out all the friends Percy had. "I'd like to have as many," the judge said before declaring judgment.

While Percy was behind bars, his wife and daughter faithfully worshipped at White Oak Baptist Church. The *Post* snapped a picture of them smiling in their pretty dresses, badges proudly clipped to their chests. *"Their badges show they're keeping up with the family's Sunday-school attendance record,"* read the caption.

Dark-haired Delma Flowers was Percy's wife—they'd been childhood sweethearts—and she was left to manage both the farm and store while he was in jail. "I'm not a bit nervous," she told the *Post*. "The Lord has his hands around me."

Percy and Delma had learned to lean on their faith. They worried about their son's passion for flying—and also forbade him from drinking alcohol. In 1952 Percy Jr. was studying law at the University of North Carolina when he took a friend's small plane for a spin. He was killed when it crashed.

Percy himself died in 1982 at the age of seventy-nine. Even before his death, his wife and daughter worried about who would eventually take care of all their land and fretted over future expenses. Daughter Becky, blonde and curly haired, had been a schoolteacher, and she struck upon an ambitious plan.

This one was legal and long term. She began converting her family's land from crops to homes. Johnston County was still rural, but she added conveniences and built neighborhoods, and over time thousands of

families moved in. The award-winning Flowers Plantation became the largest planned housing development in the entire Research Triangle.

It was also home to a convenience store.

The Percy Flowers Store is instantly recognizable on Highway 42. You can't miss it, in part because it doesn't look anything like a convenience store but rather like a stately brick home. Becky had the structure built in 1986 and modeled it after a toy store in Williamsburg, Virginia. The building is big and wide, architecturally pristine, crisp, with clean lines and immaculate grounds. Eight windows line the front, each neatly accented with a green awning. Above them, eight dormer windows perch along the slanted roof, their frames painted as white as the billowy clouds, while twin chimneys stand silhouetted against the sky.

There's a majestic symmetry about the place, except for a boxy addition that juts from the building's left side with a short white fence in front that adds a decorative touch. And yet the little building is a bit out of place because of its yellow siding next to the main building's fancy brick. Or perhaps it's not out of place at all. The addition is a liquor store, state owned and operated, taxes charged on every bottle bought.

The whole complex is eye-catching, main building and all, because it sits alone at a major intersection—NC 42 and Buffalo Road—and because of the green-and-white sign above the door that stretches nearly as wide as the windows do and reads "The Percy Flowers Store."

Percy actually built two stores at this same crossroads. When the first one burned, he erected another and ran it for years, but it was bulldozed after he died and up sprang the current one. Percy would likely tip his hat at the place. First, because it looks impressive; second, because of its bustling business; and third, because the hot dogs are famous. And almost famous.

Robert loves a convenience store. Diet Coke and pork rinds for the road, or Gatorade and a Moon Pie. Me, I'm always a little wary because the coffee, sitting stock still in the pot, tends to look thick and oily, and I just can't dare myself to spring for a cup.

I was wary when we pulled up to the Percy Flowers Store, but not because I feared the quality of the coffee—I figured a place like this brewed theirs in individual pods. No, it was more the Percy Flowers reputation that had me antsy, not to mention the fiercely protective family he'd left behind. His daughter Becky ruled the Flowers Plantation, and I'd heard she disliked the media, which, of course, couldn't get enough of a good legend. The king was dead, but years later his folklore still flourished.

There were so many rumors about the man and the operation he'd built. Somebody once told me if you crossed him, Percy might not shoot you, but somebody else would. I'd also heard of his passion for cockfighting: chickens fitted with metal spurs, ripping each other apart in a ring. He was apparently a big-time gambler who drove fancy cars and thrilled at outwitting the law and would often track the trackers tracking him.

I thought of him as a gun-toting, tobacco-chewing, no-nonsense lover of Dixie and hellion to anyone who got in his way. But then Robert told me another story about him. Years ago, Robert said his neighbor had a flat tire late one night on a rural road with no spare in the trunk. He was stranded. But then a car pulled up, and the shadow inside asked what was wrong before driving away. Fifteen minutes later, the shadow returned with a brand-new tire, said not to worry about it, "No payment needed, it's yours." The grateful neighbor caught a glimpse of the man behind the wheel and instantly recognized the face. Most everyone in eastern North Carolina knew it, for the face had often appeared in the papers. The King of the Moonshiners made for good copy.

The Good Samaritan Percy and Bootlegger Percy were both banging around my head as Robert and I walked through the door of the store that bore his name.

A convenience store is all it was, nothing quite as grand as the outside promised. It was bright inside, fluorescent lights and aisles stocked with everyday items: canned goods and motor oil, aspirin and Nabs. Coolers lined the back wall, full of soft drinks, beer, and bottled water. *Percy Flowers drinking a $2 bottled water?* That banged around my head, too. I couldn't make it fit.

But the hot dogs—now that I could see, him scarfing one in two bites and ordering a couple more from the nice ladies behind the counter. No, not just another convenience store. the Grocery Bag added a delectable dimension.

That's what it was called, the Grocery Bag, a business within a business, a hot dog stand inside the store. The grill stretched from the front door to the far wall with eight women forming a fun assembly line: steaming dogs, heating rolls, scooping chili and onions, squirting ketchup and mustard, beautifully preparing and happily serving piping red Bright Leaf hot dogs. By the time I arrived, the Grocery Bag had sold six million dogs and counting since 1983.

"Number twenty-six!" came a shout from the assembly line.

"Three all the way with cheese!"

"Number thirty-two!"

"It gets very busy," one of the ladies told me without looking up. Instead, she puffed a stray hair from her face and ladled gobs of chili onto five dogs in front of her. "One person at each station," she said. Hers was obviously the chili station, and her aim was true; not a single bean spilled, even when the pesky strand wandered into view again. "Works perfectly," she added. "It flows. Everyone has their own job." I wondered if all five dogs were bound for one person and swallowed hard.

But it wasn't time for me to eat yet. There was work to do, action to capture: the ladies, the dogs, the customers. Before I knew it, I'd forgotten all about the notorious Percy Flowers and his protective kin. My anxiety vanished like a naked dog piled high.

"Two all the way!" came another shout. I even forgot we were in the middle of a convenience store, for the Grocery Bag was an island unto itself.

"Number thirty-three!"

Robert soon abandoned the big camera and grabbed the GoPro instead. That way, he could jump in the middle of the maelstrom without whacking anybody. And sure enough, he squeezed behind the counter with all those busy ladies, jostling between them and even over them, swinging the little camera above his head for a wide-eyed panorama.

The ladies were fantastic, most in their twenties and thirties, black visors on their heads and each clad in T-shirts emblazoned with "Home of the Almost Famous Hot Dog." But the menu listed more than dogs. "We hand-roll our burgers every day," said the burger-station lady. I watched her press patties and drape them with slices—and swallowed again when the cheese oozed down the sides.

"It's quite a story," Tommy Fitzgerald told me. He owns the place, and I finally corralled him into a booth, the "booth" being a simple wooden bench with a table. Tommy was sixtyish with salt-and-pepper hair and a quick grin. He told me he started the Grocery Bag five miles down the road in 1972, a combination country store, tire business, and lawn-mower-repair shop. Percy Flowers himself used to come in and joke and tell Tommy, "Why not give it up, run mine instead?" But for ten years, Tommy struggled along. And then Percy died, and what was going to happen to the Percy Flowers Store? Tommy took a chance, reached out, signed a lease, and began running it in 1982.

"So you knew Percy?"

Tommy nodded. "Quite legendary. Where he started, where he came from, barefoot farm boy, what he did. Percy had a notoriety about him, yes he did."

I gathered "notoriety" was a kind of catchword, figured Tommy thought it best not to mention moonshine with Percy's daughter still running the plantation. Here came my skittishness again. I wasn't sure how much to ask, and Tommy was probably struggling with how much to say. "He knew who his friends were and who his enemies were," he added and left it at that.

Although he did fetch me a copy of that *Saturday Evening Post* with KING OF THE MOONSHINERS spread across the page, and he pointed to all the pictures of Percy. One showed him in a scuffle after being arrested for speeding: Percy, hat on, arms flailing, face twisted. It looked like police were trying to shove him into a car, while news photographers surrounded him. Poor Percy was outnumbered, and I found myself pulling for him to punch somebody in the nose.

Tommy showed me other photos: Percy on his farm, with his wife and dogs. "He raised world-champion fox hounds," Tommy said. "He was a good steward to the land. Took care of the poor. A nice guy." I wondered if "nice" was a catchword, too.

"Why is the hot dog almost famous?" I asked—I'd also been pondering the "almost."

Tommy's grin grew. "That's a good question," he said and told me about buying a hot dog steamer and Crock-Pot shortly after taking over the store. He threw some chili in the pot and thought he'd give it a go, and before long a man came in and ordered.

"They any good?" the man asked.

"Why, these hot dogs are almost famous," Tommy said, and the name stuck. And the dogs sold.

I ordered a couple before I left, two all the way with extra mustard, and chatted with the cashier, by far the oldest lady in the assembly line. Edna

must have been in her seventies, although the other ladies didn't call her Edna. They called her Mama Duck. "Because I try to take care of everybody," she said when I asked.

Mama Duck sure didn't dawdle. She rang the register and changed money quick as lightning—though not white lightning. "Oh, I love it. Love people." She told me she'd worked at the Grocery Bag for twenty years.

"Why so long?"

"'Cause it was in God's plan, and there are good people here to work with. Not enough positive this day and time. Life is short. You got to enjoy your life."

I marveled at how she could talk and count at the same time, one customer after another. "They worked with me through two brain tumors, so I'm mighty blessed."

That surprised me, and I asked how her health was now, and she said great. "Amen!" Putting smiles on people's faces is what she was meant to do, she said, and I found *myself* smiling, especially when she leaned over and gave me a hug.

"They're my family," Tommy said, waving at all the ladies behind the counter, meaning they felt like family. I sensed there was a bond between them born out of love and loyalty, from working hard and watching each other's backs, and I felt sure all that had started with Percy Flowers. Those traits had run down the line—and now, down the assembly line.

Percy Flowers, I mused and found my impression of the man had become even muddier than before. *Outlaw or folk hero?* It was hard to know just what was true; the man and the myth were so tightly entangled. But then, the past was past. Moonshine was out, hot dogs were in. I had only myself to trust; I could be sure only of what I could see—and what I could taste.

I gobbled down my dogs, each one in two big bites—like Percy might have done—and was tempted to order more. And another hug from Edna would have been a comfort, too. She and the other ladies were amazing, the way they worked and laughed and joked and blew stray hair out of their eyes and kept on going.

"Three all the way!"

"One with cheese and onions!"

"Two, extra ketchup!"

"We try to be known as the friendliest convenience store anywhere," Tommy said. "When you walk in the Grocery Bag, you are somebody."

"Amen!" said Mama Duck.

HIDDEN STORIES

There are certain towns in North Carolina full of intriguing stories. Murfreesboro, for example. The first time I visited that small town in the northern part of the state, I went simply to do a story on a popular lunch spot. What fun I had at Walter's Grill—and what a great cheeseburger, too.

I was mid-chew when Betsy swung by my booth. She owned the grill with her husband, who at the time was busy behind the counter grilling other cheeseburgers. I was already thinking about ordering a second one when Betsy began peppering me with other story ideas in town.

She told me the inventor of the famous Gatling gun had been from Murfreesboro and that his brother, also an inventor, had actually built the first airplane in America. "Yes," she said with hand on hip and head nodding. "Even before the Wright Brothers." I swallowed. She had my attention.

Then there was the man who had traveled the world collecting everything from mousetraps to bedpans. She told me the whole enormous collection took up three floors of an old school-turned-museum around the corner. *Bedpans?* I thought.

She mentioned a witch doctor from Murfreesboro who'd been known nationwide for his makeshift medicines and miraculous cures. And there was the little-known black baseball team, the Cornfield Boys, that trounced everyone they played, including sluggers from the major leagues who'd rolled into town with confident smirks and rolled out with their tails between their legs.

Betsy also talked about the long history of moonshine in Murfreesboro, and she told me I couldn't leave town without catching a ride on the little two-car ferry that crossed the Meherrin River. The ferry carried just two cars at a time, and she described the delightful two-minute trip from bank to bank.

When she finally finished talking, I thanked her for all the ideas then excused myself and bothered her husband for another cheeseburger to go. And, what the heck, "Throw in a hot dog all the way with extra mustard," I said.

I popped into Walter's Grill over the next several months, because I kept returning to town to do all those stories Betsy had mentioned. I even wrote about some of them in one of my previous books, *Tar Heel Traveler Eats.* Of course, I included Walter's Grill, too—I do love a good cheeseburger. And a good story.

The section that follows features North Carolina towns and counties blessed with a bevy of stories, both fascinating and surprising. Who would have known? I didn't until I went there myself and met friendly people who educated me—and sometimes fed me.

I greatly enjoyed those visits—the food, the people, the places—communities rich with hidden gems, distinctive landmarks, colorful personalities, and in many cases, little-known history. So much history. The places surprised me.

And stories with surprises are often the best kind.

MOUNT AIRY

MAYBERRY AND MORE

"Okay now, you ready to go?"

"Ready or not," I said. Actually, I *was* ready. This was going to be fun. Great characters make for great stories, and one sat in front of me, a uniformed deputy, badge pinned to his shirt, cap perched on his head, hands gripped to the wheel of a '67 Ford. "Number-one rule is to obey all rules," he said in a nasally, over-the-top impersonation of—"Nip it!"—Barney Fife.

We rolled down the main street of Mount Airy, and every head turned. How often do folks see a black-and-white squad car with a single fat siren light on the roof, big loopy antenna by the trunk, and proud gold stars on the sides? "Nip it!" My driver-deputy hollered out his window to the delight

of onlookers who pointed and laughed. "All right now, no jaywalking!" His shrilly squeal was all Barney Fife. "Move it, move it, move it!"

Don was his name, and how ironic. The actor who played Barney on *The Andy Griffith Show* was also named Don—and both Dons played a mighty good Barney. My Barney shot me a goofy, google-eyed glance from his rearview. "Now remember," he said through his nose, "when you're in Mayberry, I—am—in—control."

I loved *The Andy Griffith Show* as a kid and watched it years later in reruns. The real Andy Griffith grew up in Mount Airy and became an actor. When his show debuted in the early 1960s, he supposedly modeled the fictional town of Mayberry after his hometown of Mount Airy, although today, it's as if it's the other way around.

"Citizens arrest, citizens arrest!" Don squealed out the window, citing a famous funny line from an episode. "Nip it in the bud!" That was a famous one, too.

We rolled by Snappy Lunch, home of the pork chop sandwich; Snappy and the sandwich both had been mentioned on the show. And there was Floyd's Barber Shop and the Bluebird Diner, all here in Mount Airy just as they had been in Mayberry.

"Barney was always talking to Juanita at the Bluebird," Don said in his normal Don voice. But then we pulled up to some people at the crosswalk, and he couldn't resist. Out went his head again. "Don't be loitering now!" he hollered and laughed, and so did the crosswalkers.

Robert was also in the squad car, in the backseat with me, rolling on every hilarious Barney-ism. "Nip it!" Except every time Don squealed through his nose, Robert jiggled the camera, because he couldn't keep from laughing. Fortunately, he'd taped a GoPro to the dash—with extra duct-tape to keep it steady.

We'd shot many stories in Mount Airy over the years, many of them having nothing at all to do with *The Andy Griffith Show*, and yet the show was what brought tourists to town. "People from all over the world," Don said. "I mean, we've had them here from Australia." He stuck out his chin, and now he sounded like Crocodile Dundee. "I say, old chap!"

It was a sunny spring day, and people in shorts and T-shirts strolled up and down the sidewalk. They held hands and window shopped outside stores with colorful awnings. Tucked beneath one awning was a loudspeaker playing the show's theme song, and I could hear people whistling the tune. Then, spotting our look-alike squad car from the show, they stopped and gaped and even bounced on their toes, waving as we passed. "I mean, they're overwhelmed when they come here," Don said. "Overwhelmed. They say, 'Is that where Andy lived? Is this where . . . ?' They want to see everything. They want to reflect back on the days when things were simple."

Who could blame them? I had traveled to Mount Airy many times myself because of *The Andy Griffith Show*. I'd covered the Mayberry Days Festival, for example, which was like an annual reunion, and I had interviewed some of the actors from the show. Sadly, the actors were dying off, and I suppose in that way Mount Airy was *not* like Mayberry.

In fact, the more time I spent in Mount Airy, the more I began to think outside the box—outside the television box—and in doing so, I discovered an identity apart from Mayberry. On the surface, that seemed just about impossible, for Mount Airy was so closely linked with Mayberry. And yet in time, I learned Mount Airy was a town with colorful characters all its own. It was just a matter of looking beyond the television show, and once I did, I discovered fascinating stories in the corners of the frame.

It was then I realized Mount Airy was a town with so many other sights to see.

MOUNT AIRY

THE GRANITE QUARRY

I needed my sunglasses. All I could see was a vast expanse of bright white.

It was midsummer, and I stood in the center of the world's largest open-faced granite quarry. "Astronauts, when they're in outer space, they can actually see the quarry," said the foreman. "They can pick it out from space."

I could believe it; shielding my sunglasses-shielded eyes, I sure could—and while shielding, I was wishing I'd sprung for Ray-Bans instead of my dollar store pair.

It was strange standing in such a place, almost like being in the middle of a white desert. Nothing but endless white granite. "If you fly over the

quarry in the summertime, it's like going through a thunderstorm with all the radiant heat coming off the rock," the foreman said.

The quarry covered sixty acres on the outskirts of Mount Airy. Crews had been mining it for more than a hundred years, since 1889, and had barely scratched the surface. There was stone buried eight thousand feet below ground.

"The geologists tell us it was once a molten mass that slowly migrated to the surface of the earth," said Carlos, a vice president at the North Carolina Granite Corporation. I interviewed him outside his office building overlooking the quarry pit. Carlos wore sunglasses, too. "At one time there were mountains on top of this quarry the size of the Blue Ridge."

Below us, I saw giant blocks of granite, strewn here and there like Lincoln logs despite their monstrous size and weight, and wondered how workers moved them. Some were shaped like perfect rectangles, and I asked how they cut them. "With water," he said.

"Water?"

"The water comes out of the nozzle at forty thousand pounds per square inch, and it cuts this hard granite. Nothing but water."

He explained that Mount Airy granite had been used in monuments all over the country, including the Wright Brothers Memorial at Kitty Hawk and World War Two Memorial in D.C. "I think half of Washington is built with this granite. All the curbing in Washington is our stone."

Nothing went to waste. Even scrap pieces were crushed into grit for chickens. "Chickens have no teeth, and that gravel goes to the gizzard and becomes the teeth of the chicken. The rock and the gravel grind the corn."

"Fascinating," I told him. "And here in Mount Airy." Carlos nodded.

Robert and I braved the heat and blinding bright white as long as we could—I think he had to use a filter on his camera lens. In spite of my sore eyes, I told the foreman I was impressed, and we both took a moment to gaze over the granite landscape. He sighed and finally spoke, and when he did, he enunciated each word. "The largest open-faced granite quarry in the world."

He sounded rather proud, though I did wonder about that rather heavy sigh. It may have been from the heat or from exhaustion, I couldn't tell.

But at least he wore thick sunglasses.

Don the deputy pointed out all the granite buildings in town. "Made with Mount Airy stone," he said. "That one, too." I think he was having a ball playing tour guide to the media folks from Raleigh. "When I grew up, we didn't have television. I had to watch the radio," he said and laughed.

He'd been driving a Mayberry squad car for a decade, one of several drivers the local tour company used; there were multiple Barney Fifes in

town driving identical cars, although I couldn't imagine any Barney being as entertaining as ours—except maybe for the one on *The Andy Griffith Show*.

We turned down a residential street and rolled to a stop in front of a small plain house. "That's where Andy grew up," Don said. The house was yellow with brown shutters, a brown roof, and an overhang over the front door. A two-bedroom, one-bath little place that stayed booked, Don said. A sign in the yard listed phone numbers to call for lodging reservations, and he said I wouldn't believe the number of people willing to pay un-Mayberry-like sums for the privilege.

We sat looking at the house for a while, seeing nothing in particular. And yet, knowing this was Andy Griffith's house had a certain mesmerizing allure. When we finally pulled away, Don glanced at me in the rearview and smiled. "Simple days," he said.

MOUNT AIRY

THE MOONSHINE MONK

The simple life . . .

For twenty-five years, Vann McCoy was a monk. Then he became a moonshiner.

On one of my trips to Mount Airy, I had visited Mayberry Spirits Distillery and met Vann McCoy, the energetic man who opened it. He was nearing fifty at the time, bald-headed, and seemed to enjoy playing up his monastic past versus his moonshine profession. "I like to think it's all about lifting your spirit," he said, tilting his head toward the heavens.

It was legal moonshine, of course. "Sorghum whiskey," he said, holding up a glass jug. "Beautiful iced tea kind of look." It did look like iced tea, except his version was a hundred proof. "Refreshing on a nice afternoon."

We were in a back room full of barrels, bottles, and tubes, a potent yeasty smell heavy in the air. "The steam will rise through these chambers," he said, pointing to copper containers stacked above a large round vat. "The yeast meets the sugar to create alcohol."

I nodded but wasn't entirely interested in the nitty gritty. What I wanted to know was why he became a monk and how he went from monk to moonshiner. Vann smiled when I asked, as though he'd heard the question a thousand times—no doubt he had.

He grew up in Mount Airy, he told me, and had always been curious about how things worked. In college, he began studying astrophysics but soon felt another pull, an even greater curiosity, a shift from intricate earthly matters to the mysteries of the spiritual world.

"I decided to study the heavens instead of the stars," he said and smiled and tilted his head again—he'd apparently also spent time studying the odd dynamics of his life.

He eventually became a Cistercian monk. "It's a beautiful life," he said, this time keeping his eyes on mine. "You learn about yourself, the dark within." He did not elaborate on the dark, but did so on the joy he shared with his fellow monks and in the life he had chosen.

It was not an entirely quiet life. Vann started several businesses on the monastery's behalf, including office supply and coffee companies, even a dog biscuit venture. The profits helped support charities, along with the monks themselves, who believed in self-sufficiency.

Before long, Vann was traveling the world, giving speeches and business advice to entrepreneurs. "I even had a plane and was a flying monk," he told me. It was a unique role, for most monks are, in his words, "stay-put monks," and yet he was one who stayed on the go.

Most monks don't usually retire, either—once a monk, always a monk—but in time, Vann did retire; he stepped down as leader of his monastery and went on sabbatical, spending quiet days in Ireland.

Around that time, back home in Mount Airy, his mother wasn't doing so well, and when Vann returned for a visit, he felt another call: to stay home and take care of her until she was "smiling on the other side." He didn't know how long that would be or if he would ever go back to his monastic life. "It was an open question."

It was one that also posed a problem. He would need a job. "My thought was, seeing where craft beers were going at the time, that distilleries would be the next thing to happen." It was a logical choice. Distilling, brewing, and wine making are monastic traditions; some monasteries have practiced them for a thousand years.

Vann's own experience with alcohol began when he was thirteen. He attended a camp on Appalachian culture, learned about moonshine, came home, and gathered up his mom's pressure cooker and some copper pipe and hauled them to the porch. He was in the midst of concocting his first batch when she walked in on him. But instead of scolding him, she laughed and shook her head and probably figured it was only a matter of time. She told young Vann his entire family had been making moonshine for 150 years.

Vann had come a long way since then—or maybe not. I wondered just how different his pressure-cooker experiment on the porch had been from his contraption operation in the back room of his store. Except Mayberry Spirits was clearly not some fly-by-night, makeshift whim. He sold his award-winning moonshine in ABC stores across the state and had plans to expand beyond North Carolina.

He soon led me from the back of the store to the front section, and what a whole different atmosphere. The room was impressive, full of fine wood and warm, earthy tones. Crisp bottles of moonshine were everywhere, creatively displayed on tables and crates. The clean, catchy labels read MAYBERRY RFD, which of course was the official name of the town in *The Andy Griffith Show*. But in this case, "RFD" meant "Really Fine Drink." That was printed on the label, too, circled in red ink.

Mayberry Spirits also sells gifts, including jewelry from Asheville artists and hand-rolled cigars marinated with whiskey. The store caters to tourists, and Vann clearly enjoys mingling with folks and entertaining his audience. At one point, I stood on my toes listening in, and when he got to the monk part, he suddenly turned his back. Nobody was sure what was happening, and people began craning their necks to see. Then at last, he spun around, wearing a long gray beard that stretched all the way to his waist, and delivered the line about lifting people's spirits. The audience howled, and I did, too, even though I'd heard the joke before—and even though I wasn't sure whether he was trying to look like an ancient monk or hard-core hillbilly. Or maybe both.

He also spoke to the group about spreading love and inspiring others. "And if you make a good product, all the better," he said. "What's more American than apple pie and whiskey from Mayberry?"

I actually sampled some myself, a few small sips, and it was mighty smooth. And so was Vann. He was an expert at contrasting his monastic life with his moonshine profession. He lifted a shot glass and offered a toast. "It's good for the soul. It will make your eyes twinkle and help your heart open up a little more."

He smiled, swirled the 'shine, and tilted his head toward the heavens.

MOUNT AIRY

THELMA LOU

"Don't be loitering now!" Don the deputy hollered from the squad car. Between Don and the Moonshine Monk, I was beginning to think Mount Airy was full of people hamming it up and playing a role. "Nip it!" he said for the tenth time and laughed.

When he settled down, I asked if he'd ever run into Betty Lynn, the actress who played Thelma Lou, Barney's girlfriend on *The Andy Griffith Show*. Don said he'd seen her around and that she was always friendly.

I understood Betty Lynn loved her role as Thelma Lou. In fact, she had loved *The Andy Griffith Show* so much she eventually moved to Mount Airy, the closest thing to Mayberry, and it had all worked out; the real-life town had been a suitable substitute for the fictional one.

Betty was one of the few regulars from the show still living. I had interviewed her in Mount Airy on her ninetieth birthday, and she never stopped smiling. She wore a flowered dress for the occasion, and after all these years, her red hair was still red—though a much lighter shade than her lipstick.

"I'm just the luckiest person I know," she said, sitting at a table in front of an adoring crowd that had lined up to shake her hand and receive an autographed picture. "It's emotional, their feeling about the show, and I'm here to receive all that, I guess."

She was full of emotion herself; Betty's voice was on the edge of breaking. "Mount Airy is like Mayberry in a lot of ways. It's very sweet."

The picture she signed and handed out was black and white but "colorful" nonetheless. It was one of her planting a smooch on Barney's cheek, big-eyed Barney looking absolutely befuddled. The rest of his face was covered in kisses, too, fat lipstick marks from cheek to cheek, smooches everywhere.

As for Betty, she still had those same sparkling eyes. And now, almost half a century later, her fans still loved her; the line to greet her was out the door. To them, I supposed Betty Lynn would always be Thelma Lou.

She stopped signing for a moment and addressed her fans. "Everything about that show was so good and still is. It meant everything to me." She put her hand on her heart, and I thought for a moment this was it, she was going to cry. "I'm so grateful." She looked down at the picture, at Thelma Lou and Barney, Barney with all his kisses, and I felt in that moment she was longing for those days again, those lovely, funny, simple days. But then she looked up again. "And I'm happy I'm ninety," she said and smiled through watery eyes.

After a little while, somebody brought out a cake and everyone joined in to sing happy birthday. Even Betty clapped when it was over and then went back to signing pictures. People in line seemed content just to stand and watch her, several of them misty-eyed themselves. And many put a hand over *their* hearts, too.

MOUNT AIRY

DISC GOLF AND THE STORY OF GEORGE

One story leads to another. And another.

I had first met Betty Lynn by way of George Sappenfield. Betty and George were friends, and it was George who drove her to a media dinner one night. I sat at a table with other reporters while Betty entertained us with tales about her acting career. She was not yet ninety then, and I was already planning to cover her upcoming birthday celebration. So, at one point, I broke off and chatted with George.

He was a Californian with a ruddy face and mop of gray hair. He had settled in Surry County a decade before and worked at the community college. He was happy to talk and thrilled when I said I wanted to do a story on him—I'd been told who he was. I picked the date, and he picked the place. "I'll bring plenty of Frisbees," he said.

George Sappenfield was the inventor of Frisbee golf or disc golf—or one of the inventors; the game's history is blurry, but George had certainly made a name for himself. I'd Googled his name, and it immediately popped up. And now here he was in Mount Airy.

Robert and I met him a few weeks later on a crisp winter day near his home on a disc-golf course. "You know, there's over five thousand courses now," he said. George had designed about thirty courses himself. "Every country has one. Every continent."

The place he'd picked for us was a wide, green, rolling landscape, much like a golf course, but edged by woods, which were part of the course, too. He pointed to targets between trees. I had never played the game and asked him to demonstrate—preferably on the spacious, treeless part of the course.

George had obviously come ready to play. He wore jeans and a sweatshirt and pulled a Frisbee from a lumpy canvas bag. After a few practice pumps of his wrist, he flung the disc at a basket a short distance away. The basket was attached to a metal pole with chains around it—sort of like a waist-high basketball hoop in a flimsy jail cell. The Frisbee sailed wide, as did the next toss, and the next. George hung his head and admitted he was rusty then took a few steps closer. Bingo! This time it broke through the loose chains and landed in the basket, and Robert caught it all on camera. George beamed. But to me, the best part was not the shot but the sound. I'd clipped a microphone to the pole, which beautifully captured the reverberating rattle and clang.

George told me how it all started; I think he was glad to—he'd been working up a sweat.

It began on a Friday afternoon in 1965. He was playing a round of golf but found himself thinking instead about his job. He'd been working as a recreation counselor in Fresno during his summer break from college. On the fairway that afternoon, he kept thinking about the park he'd been assigned to and especially one area that was rarely used. As a rec counselor, he'd been taught to take advantage of every available space and piece of equipment. It pained him a bit to think about the hula hoops and Frisbees collecting cobwebs in the park's supply shed. And that's when the idea struck—perhaps at the very moment he struck the golf ball. "Well, shoot," he said to himself, "I'll just set up a little Frisbee golf."

The next day he carried some wooden stakes with him to the park and drove them into the ground, then he collected the hula hoops from the

shed and tied them to the posts. Next he gathered up the Frisbees, rounded up the kids, and explained the object of the game: Begin at the starting point, throw the Frisbee as far and accurately as you can, then pick it up and toss it again, closing in on the hoop, and finally fling it through the hoop—just like golf where the player hits the ball closer and closer to the hole until he sinks it—and around the course we go. The kids loved it, and George was tickled, too, and from then on he continued to set up his Frisbee/hula hoop/golf course each month at the park.

A few years later, George had graduated from college and was still teaching and playing the game while working full-time as a recreation supervisor. He thought it might be fun to hold a Frisbee-golf tournament, though he knew he would need lots of hula hoops and Frisbees. He contacted the California-based Wham-O company about donating them. Wham-O had been selling both products since the late 1950s but had begun to think about marketing Frisbees not as toys but as sporting goods—if only it could invent some competitive Frisbee games. That's about the time George came calling. "A perfect storm kind of thing," he said. The company execs perked up and not only supplied what he needed for the tournament, but also sent a P.R. man to check it out.

George held his tournament in May 1969. Wham-O had been planning a Frisbee tournament of its own, though it would be a contest judged mainly on how far players could throw and the tricks they could do. George convinced the company to include Frisbee golf as well, despite the skepticism of one of its managers. Six months later, Wham-O's nine-hole competition in Pasadena became a historic milestone, the first professional Frisbee-golf tournament ever held.

The company felt it was on to something and hired George as a consultant. It was George who organized Wham-O's National Hula Hoop and Frisbee competitions for youth; he even wrote the rules.

Disc golf was beginning to take shape. Soon, out went hula hoops tied to posts and in went sturdy metal baskets. And who developed those baskets? The skeptical manager at Wham-O who'd sneered at the idea of including Frisbee golf in the company tournament. Ironically enough, he left the company to make his living off the game, and a good living, too. In fact, Ed Headrick is often called the Father of Disc Golf—rightly or wrongly.

George led Robert and I to his car and grabbed a folder from the backseat, leaned against the trunk, and riffled through a stack of newspaper clippings. He plucked out an old black-and-white photo in which his hair was a much thicker mop. It was a freeze frame of him and Dinah Shore,

taken from her popular daytime talk show. I remembered Dinah Shore as a kid; my mom used to watch her all the time. "I mean, that's national television," I said.

"Yeah, it was kind of surreal."

He showed me other pictures, George posing with singer Kenny Rogers and with actor Larry Hagman. "Every time Larry directed an episode of *Dallas,* there was a Frisbee in it," he said and told me Hagman was a huge fan of the game.

George also handed me a comic book, and there he was, illustrated on the page tossing a Frisbee. The book was a Special Olympics publication—and here was yet another story.

Back when disc golf was taking off, George would hold demonstrations at schools, including schools with special-needs kids. The children would often miss the hole but seemed to have just as much fun running after their errant Frisbees. One teacher exclaimed, "I've never seen that child run before!" She never knew the child could.

George ended up working for International Special Olympics in the late 1970s, teaming with Eunice Kennedy Shriver, who founded the organization and who was also the sister of President John F. Kennedy. The comic book was a Special Olympics coaches' guide and training manual. The artist who illustrated George was the same one who'd drawn Superman comics.

I stood in the parking lot so long while listening to George's fascinating background that I began to feel the winter chill and suggested we head back to the course for more video. I'd also seen a few cars pull in, which surprised me since it was midday, midweek, mid-February. But when we returned to the course, several people were playing—and playing like they meant it; I bet they weren't chilly at all.

I interrupted a high school kid who told me it was a teacher workshop day, though I think his teachers would have been proud. He seemed to be studying hard during his time off. He trained his eyes on the woods ahead and aimed his Frisbee like a golfer gauging the next critical putt. "Right here we have a mando tree," he explained. "That's mandatory. You have to go around to the left of it." He rotated his wrist, slowly waving the disc back and forth, and finally let it fly.

It rose in a high sideways arc, missing the trunk by inches, and then, curiously, curled around the tree, propelled by some wizardly spin, and landed in leaves on the opposite side, in direct line-of-sight of the basket.

"Amazing," I said, but the kid merely smiled and shrugged and went tromping through the woods to retrieve it and plot the next throw.

I interviewed another player, a few years older, who told me he was taking a break from work, although he looked to be carrying a hefty briefcase. He set it down and pulled it open and showed me at least twenty discs neatly tucked in separate compartments. "Different weights," he said and explained how important it was to choose the right one for the right shot.

Even George could hardly believe how the game had progressed. "Here it is," he said, looking down at the disc in his hands. "This little piece of plastic helped me get out in the world."

It also helped get him into the *World Book Encyclopedia*, which in 1983 felt it had to address the word *Frisbee*, by then widely used. So *World Book*

included a description and a picture of George ready to show off one of his nifty sidearm tosses.

Years later, George would be voted into the International Disc Golf Hall of Fame. And that little piece of plastic did even more. It helped bring him to North Carolina.

In the early 1980s, George gave up his Wham-O consulting job, having earned his doctorate in commercial recreation by then, and took a position at East Carolina University. He enjoyed the East Coast, enjoyed North Carolina, and in 2006 moved to the Mount Airy area when Surry Community College recruited him as one of its vice presidents.

Now here he was on a disc-golf course close to his home, trying his best for the camera, tossing Frisbees at the metal basket but often missing. I told him not to worry, that we'd edit our story carefully, and he smiled and kept at it. I certainly admired his persistence, not to mention all that he'd accomplished, a man largely responsible for the invention of the game itself. And now there were more than five thousand disc-golf courses across the globe.

"It's very exciting," he said between throws, a bit out of breath. "To this day, it's always a thrill for me to see people playing disc golf."

He tossed and missed but smiled again for the camera. "Boy, what a great day to be out on the disc golf course," he said and pulled another Frisbee from his not-so-lumpy bag anymore. "Now if I can just get it in the basket, it'll be even more fun." He laughed and flung it, and—bingo! Bingo at last.

Rattle and clang.

MOUNT AIRY

"THE HAPPIEST GIRL IN THE WHOLE USA"

I had a feeling Don the deputy was stretching the squad-car tour. We'd been bumping along for close to an hour, and I think he enjoyed having the television camera as a passenger.

"Don't think I could live anywhere else," he said. "It's . . ." He clamped his bottom lip over his top one and grappled for the right word. "Decent," he finally said. "It's decent."

I asked him if he'd ever met Donna Fargo, the famous country singer from Mount Airy, and half-expected him to start singing her signature song, "The Happiest Girl in the Whole USA." I also wondered what the tourists would think if he sang it in his Barney voice.

I remembered singing the song myself when I was a kid. It came out when I was ten, and it had a fun, joyful beat—though when I sang it, I usually changed the words to "I'm the happiest *boy* in the whole USA."

Don said he hadn't met Donna. She lived in California now, but he knew about her; he had to because tourists sometimes asked—or at least the ones who had done their Mount Airy research. I had researched Donna Fargo myself in hopes of landing an interview in case she ever returned home. I was impressed to see her listed alongside stars such as Loretta Lynn, Dolly Parton, and Tammy Wynette. *Billboard Magazine* had named her one of the most successful female country artists of the 1970s.

I was surprised to learn Donna had been diagnosed with multiple sclerosis near the height of her career, and yet, she continued to turn out songs and wrote most of her own material.

What an inspiring story, I thought, and the more I thought about it, the more I told myself I should try to contact Donna and see if she might return to Mount Airy for a visit. If so, maybe I could interview her and do a story. If not, maybe I could interview her anyway and learn more of her story.

"I trusted the dream. I've always thought dreams were gifts from God, and it's our responsibility to try to make them come true."

That was the powerful response to one of the questions I had emailed Donna. I couldn't wait to read the rest.

Donna's good friend from Mount Airy had given me her contact information, so I called Donna in California and left a message. She called me back and did the same. It seemed we were both on the go, and so we agreed, through email, that email was best.

"Mount Airy was a fine hometown," she wrote and told me about working on her family's farm when she was a kid and having to tie tobacco leaves. I knew from interviewing old-timers that tobacco could be hot, grueling labor. "Working at such a young age fostered my independent spirit."

She ventured to California for college and, after graduating, taught school by day and by night sang in clubs—she'd been singing since she was a teenager. She met her husband while performing, and they married in 1968.

"I was happy with my life at the time," she said. "I had made my other dream come true of being a high school English teacher, so I felt a certain sense of accomplishment, and I think that background and experience fueled my imagination. So I sat down one day and started strumming the guitar."

She strummed and made up the words as she went. "Happiest girl in the world . . ." But she didn't like it; technically, *girl* and *world* didn't rhyme. "I don't like filler rhymes. I want every word to be significant."

She kept at it. "And I got the chorus. 'Shine on me, sunshine. Walk with me, world. It's a skippety do da day. I'm the happiest girl . . .' And it was clear then to finish with, 'in the whole USA.' So I limited happiness to this country rather than the whole world. Ha." I laughed, too, when I read "Ha" at the end of her sentence.

"The Happiest Girl in the Whole USA" became a smash hit in 1972, reaching number one on the country charts and number eleven on the pop charts. Her follow-up single, "Funny Face," did even better. Both songs were million-sellers. "They were certainly confirmation that I was mightily blessed by God," she wrote in her email.

She released other hit songs, won a Grammy Award, performed at the Grand Ole Opry and Carnegie Hall, and in 1978 even starred in her own syndicated television show.

And then came multiple sclerosis.

"I'm not sure I'd even heard of MS. Since they said it was incurable, I was on my own. I remember thinking, *Okay, I have this, but I'm not gonna let it have me.* And that was the attitude I kept front and center." She said the disease had twice left her paralyzed and that it was something she still struggled with today. "There are episodes that make you miserable, tacked onto the sustained discomfort, but you have to deal with the surprises you face in life."

She dealt with it first by continuing to write, record, and perform. She scored another top-ten hit the year after her diagnosis, and later started her own line of greeting cards and began writing books. I was surprised to learn she'd written seven books, even though I knew she'd been an acclaimed and prolific songwriter.

"I think writing to a writer is a way to continue to learn, because we explore the truths of life, and that's satisfying and invigorating to the soul," she told me in her email, and as a writer myself, I admired her answer.

In fact, it was rather exciting trading notes with Donna Fargo. I kept thinking about singing her song when I was a kid—and changing it. I was tempted to tell her that story in my email and write "Ha" at the end of it.

She ended her responses with those articulate thoughts on writing and exploring the truths of life and invigorating the soul. And she added one final thought, too, short and simple but powerful just the same. "If you're not happy, you're cheating yourself."

I printed out her answers, all the while humming her signature song.

Don the deputy at last pulled into Wally's Service Station, the tour's end, as well as its beginning. People were waiting in line, and other Barneys in other squad cars were ready to roll. I loved seeing those old cars, the black-and-whites with the gold stars and loopy antennas. I hadn't wanted the tour to end. Or my visit, either. Mount Airy had a charm all its own.

Robert and I thanked Don, climbed out, and began gathering our gear at the curb. "No loitering now!" he yelped through his nose. "Move it, move it!" He laughed and revved the engine, and Robert told him to wait just a minute, then scrambled behind the rear bumper and positioned the camera on the tailpipe. Don gave the engine another big rev, blowing smoke, and rolled forward. He puttered into the distance at two miles an hour, a beautiful closing shot for our story.

And the sound was perfect, too. Twenty feet down the road, he poked his head out the window. "Nip—it—in—the—bud!"

HERTFORD

CATFISH, WOLFMAN, AND MORE

Sometimes the simplest stories resonate the most.

Hertford, North Carolina, is a quaint town in the northeast corner of the state, and Sid Eley was delighted Robert and I had come for a visit. He was proud of Hertford and wanted to show it off.

Sid was a good bit older than I was, a man with wire-rimmed glasses and a white mustache who smiled after every sentence he spoke. He was head of the Chamber of Commerce, though I think the chamber consisted of just two people: Sid and a secretary. Their office was a brick building with a white porch near the town square, and the first time I walked in, the secretary actually clapped her hands. "Welcome, welcome. Sid's in back. Been expecting you," she said but didn't call out for Sid or dial his line. I guess she figured he'd heard us come in—the building wasn't much bigger than my den, although it did have a narrow hall with a couple of doors. "Think he's straightening up," she said. "Be right with you."

I took a moment to look around. The office was full of colorful brochures with pretty coastal scenes: boats, a curvy bridge, turtles lounging in the sun, and the nighttime waterfront glowing beneath a full moon. This was my first trip to Hertford; it was the early days of the Tar Heel Traveler, and as I peered at the inviting images, I actually thought this wouldn't be a bad place to retire—but no time soon. I wasn't even forty-five yet.

I plucked another brochure from the rack, this one different from the others. A rugged man in a ball cap stared back at me—and talk about mustaches; his was dark and bushy. The brochure's headline was catchy. It read CATFISH.

HERTFORD

CATFISH HUNTER

Catfish is who had brought me to Hertford in the first place: Jim Catfish Hunter, the legendary baseball player who pitched for the Oakland As and New York Yankees in the 1960s and '70s. He was an eight-time All-Star and five-time World Series champion. With his quirky name and trademark mustache, he was hard to forget. I remembered him from when I was a kid cheering for the Red Sox. With Catfish on the mound in pinstripes, I rooted against him—but not too much. I liked his name.

"See you're reading about Jimmy," came a voice. I turned to see that other mustache, the white one with the permanent smile below it that would become so familiar to me in the years ahead. Sid emerged from the hall and introduced himself. "Welcome to our town," he said and twanged

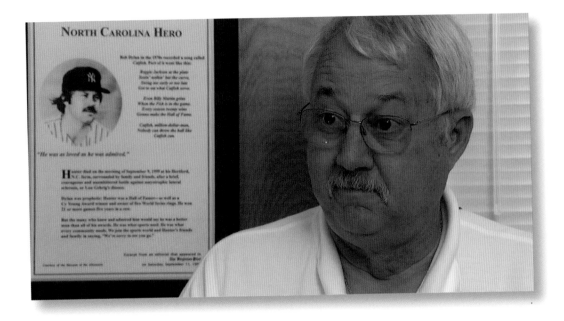

the word *town*. "Love to show you around." He also twanged *around*. The emphasis on "ow" sounds was definitely coastal North Carolina. "But first, come see our Jimmy Hunter museum."

The room down the hall was, at the time, only half the size of my den and more crowded than my coat closet (although it has greatly expanded since my visit). "The Jimmy 'Catfish' Hunter Room" was painted on the sign on the door. Inside, Catfish filled every square inch. His face was in pictures, his windup on posters, his name scrolled on baseballs and embroidered on hats and even stamped on a 45 record. Big Tom White performed "The Catfish Kid," a peppy jingle with simple lyrics: "He did a lot of pitching and had a lot of fun." I learned somebody else had recorded a song about Catfish Hunter as well: music legend Bob Dylan who penned his own version in 1975.

Sid tapped a photo on the wall showing a young man at a table with pen and paper. The clean-cut kid looked like a high schooler confronting an algebra assignment. I figured the couple looming over his shoulder must be his folks, checking his math. Sid smiled and told me Jimmy's mom and dad had to cosign his first major-league contract. "He was too young, seventeen years old." I looked closer at Catfish and marveled. No trace of a mustache whatsoever.

Jimmy Hunter graduated from Perquimans High in 1964 and went directly to the major leagues; he skipped over the minors altogether. That first contract he signed was with the A's, whose owner thought the kid needed a flashy name to go with his powerful arm. "You know, Jimmy loved to hunt and fish," Sid said. And so "Catfish" is what the world and record books would call him, but not Sid. To him, it was always Jimmy. "I tell people he was a hall of fame man who made it into the Hall of Fame."

When Sid eventually drove us around town, just about everyone we met had known Jimmy. "It seemed like he was throwing rockets," the local pharmacist said. "And an unbelievable batter. His batting average was incredible." That surprised me because I had always known Catfish Hunter as a pitcher. And yet in 1971, he pounded out thirty-six hits in thirty-eight games; I looked up his stats later.

I also read about the perfect game he pitched in 1968; at that time, just the ninth perfect game in baseball history. The game was special for another reason, too. Jimmy connected at the plate, driving in three of the A's four runs.

In 1975 Catfish became the highest-paid player in baseball when he joined the New York Yankees, signing a five-year contract worth $3.3 million. "But he never flaunted his money or his talent," Sid said and talked of watching him on national television, his good buddy from Hertford, throwing strikes in front of thousands of cheering fans.

Sid pulled up to a ten-foot-high granite stone in the center of town. It was a monument in honor of Catfish, engraved with many of his achievements:

CY YOUNG AWARD WINNER—1974
WON 20 OR MORE GAMES FIVE CONSECUTIVE YEARS
PITCHED IN SIX WORLD SERIES
INDUCTED INTO BASEBALL HALL OF FAME—1987

Catfish spent fifteen years in the majors and retired in 1979 with more than two thousand strikeouts—that statistic wasn't listed; there wasn't enough room. Then he moved back home to Hertford to hunt and fish. "He never changed," Sid said. "He was just Jimmy, always a good guy."

Sid drove us to another stone monument, shaped in part like a baseball, engraved with the Yankees' and A's insignias and *Jim 'Catfish' Hunter* scrolled in the middle between the seams. The rest of the stone was flat with "Hunter" spelled in tall letters across the front. At the monument's base, planted in the grass, was a much smaller stone that listed his full name and two dates, the second being September 9, 1999. The day he died.

He was fifty-three years old and had been diagnosed with ALS the year before. It was the same disease that took the life of another baseball great: Lou Gehrig, also a New York Yankee. Sid told me how quickly Jimmy's disease had progressed; his hands and arms were the first to go, that oh-so-powerful arm and curveball hand. But he talked more about what a hard worker he'd been. "He never let his fame go to his head. He was just Jimmy, just an old country boy. His funeral was the largest one that's ever been held here."

I admired the impressive gravestone and its unusual baseball design, how creative it was. Somebody had put a lot of thought and care into constructing it. I even admired the Yankees insignia emblazoned at the top.

I found myself wishing I had never rooted against him.

Sid was a good public relations man who drove us to other sights around Hertford, and I kept adding inventory to my notepad, thinking we'd have to come back and shoot all these other stories.

At one point, he drove us by the water and slowed almost to a stop. "Oh, by the way, that's our turtle log." I put my pen down and followed his finger to a point fifty feet from shore, and there indeed was a log sticking out of the water, not sticking straight up but resting at an angle with waves rippling just below it. It was splintered at the end and short, about three feet long, or at least the visible part was; I figured the other end had to be wedged deep into the river floor.

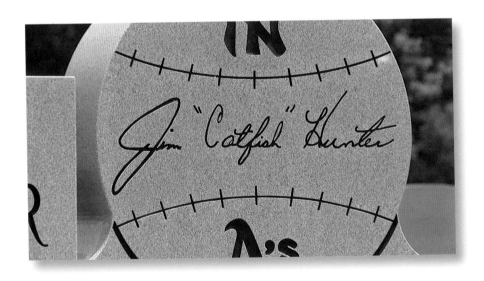

What I found so curious were three turtles resting on the log, lined one behind the other, apparently sunning themselves and enjoying a lazy afternoon. Sid said the turtle log had been around for as long as anybody could remember; it had survived hurricanes and was such a landmark that the image had been stamped on the town's seal. I asked if we could pull over for a closer look, and he happily obliged.

We stood at the bank, and at first it was like watching grass grow; in fact, the turtles' heads stood up like green blades that didn't move. Nothing moved except the water. But in time, they began stirring, stretching their skinny necks for a look around. Then, suddenly, I saw a turtle emerge from the water. Using its little legs, the scrappy fellow pulled its way onto the log, shoved itself into line, and in doing so knocked one of his buddies off. *Plop*!

I could have stood and watched all afternoon. It was just a simple little thing, but I was fascinated and pretty sure viewers would be, too.

We were due back in Raleigh, a two-hour drive home, and when we at last turned for the car, I scribbled *Turtle Log* in my notepad and even underlined it. I suppose I should have written it at the top of the page, but I merely added it to my story list. It was a long list; Sid had pitched me a number of good ideas, and I figured I'd work my way down and in time reach the turtle log.

So many stories. I felt we had to return soon and begin chipping away at them, one at a time. And so my eyes traveled up the page, up to the top, where they settled on a single word, the one that began my list.

The word I'd written was *Wolfman*.

HERTFORD

WOLFMAN JACK

Mick Jagger came to town—Mick, the super skinny, big-lipped English-man and lead singer of the Rolling Stones. I can picture him now strutting through Hertford in black leather pants, ruffled red-velvet shirt, gold chains dangling from his neck, and a half-dozen bracelets clinking on each thin wrist. I can also see people in town doing double and triple takes, especially gray-haired women with pocketbooks dangling from *their* wrists. I doubt if anyone ventured to ask Mick for an autograph. I'm sure they realized he wasn't from around those parts, but they probably had no idea who he was.

At least, I assume he came to Hertford. He practically had to in order to visit Belvidere, a little crossroads just outside of town. Word is, he definitely ventured there. That's right, Mick Jagger, the gazillionaire rocker with millions of fans worldwide, popped up in Belvidere, and maybe more than once. And yet there's almost nothing in Belvidere, just lonely stretches of road and old clapboard houses.

However, there is a supermarket, which also looks like a house, an old white one with a creaky front porch and friendly butcher inside. His name is Doug Layden; the place is Layden's Supermarket, and I watched Doug carve hunks of raw beef. Layden's is actually quite famous for its meat, and I wondered if Mick might have grabbed a couple of rib eyes. Or was Mick a vegetarian? Maybe so. But he probably would have sprung for the steaks anyway, at least two hefty ones for the buddy he came to Belvidere to visit. I can't imagine that fella was a vegetarian. No way. Not the Wolfman.

Wolfman Jack. He was the legendary DJ with the scratchy voice who howled from radio dials in '57 Chevys and who skyrocketed to rock-and-roll stardom. *American Graffiti* came out in 1973, a movie famous for its rugged nostalgia that portrayed 1950s' teens with flipped-up collars and slicked-back hair drag racing souped-up cars with the radios cranked. The Wolfman was on, and his voice was the voice of the times, full of raw power.

"Rock on, baby!" he bellowed on screen from the radio dial. "Rock and roll yourself to death! Oh, mercy!"

The movie was all fiction with make-believe characters racing their way through a thin plot. But it was a thrill; it was fun. And Wolfman Jack was real, an established disc jockey already known to thousands of hip American youngsters. He played himself in the movie and instantly became known to millions more.

"The Wolfman is everywhere," he growled on film, and I loved it. I was eleven years old when the movie debuted, and even at that age I knew I wanted a career behind a microphone. The Wolfman clued me to the power of voice and the thrill of the airwaves. *Oowwwww!*

Wolfman Jack lived the last years of his life outside Hertford in tiny Belvidere, and the few people living in Belvidere must have done double and triple takes, too, because Wolfman looked like a wolf man—a big, burly, barrel-chested guy with jet black hair that flowed to his neck and his signature salt-and-pepper goatee. He often wore a black shirt beneath a black leather jacket. And then, of course, there was the voice, deep and raspy even in everyday conversation.

"When he ordered a pound of sausage, it was, 'Gimme a pound of sausage!'" Doug said. We were standing on the creaky porch of his supermarket, and I think he was trying to sound something like an overweight hound dog with a sore throat. "He'd come by and say, 'Hey, Doug, fix me up twenty-five steaks!' He enjoyed eating. That was his thing. And he was starting to show it." Doug dropped his voice with that last bit of info, losing the bark and whispering instead.

Wolfman wound up in Belvidere after marrying a woman who'd been raised in the area. They met at one of his radio-station stops; Wolfman moved many times as his popularity grew. His smoky baritone eventually became one of the most recognizable voices in America. And in time, so did his face. *American Graffiti* had a lot to do with that. He appeared on camera in a pivotal scene—the radio DJ revealed.

He soon appeared in other movies and hobnobbed with celebrities, including Mick Jagger, while devouring celebrity status of his own—and all its evil influences. But his marriage held. In fact, Wolfman often mentioned his wife on the radio. He called her Mrs. Wolfman. *Oowww!* Their little place in Perquimans County was a quiet, comfortable getaway—with juicy rib eyes just down the road.

"People in North Carolina live real good," Wolfman once told a WRAL reporter; I found the old footage in the station archives. He was a little grayer than I'd remembered as a kid—and heavier, thanks to good eating—but still the same Wolfman. I smiled as I watched him on tape. At one point, he sniffed the air, a powerful, chest-out-all-the-way sniff, followed by an equally explosive exhale. "Real clean-livin' folks," he said.

Doug told me Wolfman had opened up to him about being Wolfman. "He said he had to protect his image."

"Do you think he felt trapped by that image?" I asked.

"Oh, yeah," Doug said and explained that that was mainly why Wolfman had moved to Belvidere. Although he didn't fade into oblivion. In fact, he built a recording studio behind his house and continued to yip and howl across the country. And entertain friends, such as Mick.

"Mick Jagger in Belvidere?" I asked Doug, and we both laughed, but he confirmed it was true. I wondered if Mick had ever stopped to admire the turtle log in Hertford, and if he did, whether it gave him a peaceful sense of . . . *SATISFACTION*.

But Doug soon quit laughing, because his friend the Wolfman was no more, his famous howl silent. He died of a heart attack at home in Belvidere in 1995 at age fifty-seven.

I found his tombstone beside his house, his birth name neatly engraved across the front: ROBERT WESTON SMITH. I wondered if he'd been a man of

faith. Two large angel statues stood on each side of the grave as if watching over it, and on the stone itself, chiseled above his name, was a cross.

If that's all I'd seen, I would have thought Robert Weston Smith had been a simple and dutiful servant of the Lord—and he may have been. But the tombstone also included "Wolfman Jack" engraved in all caps at the top, like a screaming headline. Or a howling one.

But the howl was saved for the bottom of the stone. The letters inscribed at the base read "Ooooowwww!"

HERTFORD

PERQUIMANS COUNTY COURTHOUSE

People in Raleigh tend to head for the coast on sunny weekends, hop in their cars, drive south and east to Atlantic Beach or Sunset Beach or any number of sandy getaways in between. Oak Island, Ocean Isle, Emerald Isle, etc. are all lined along the lip, kissing the Atlantic. Pick one and don't pack much: a favorite T-shirt, shorts, and flip-flops. Aren't we lucky to live in such a beautiful, laid-back state?

My trips to Perquimans County also took me to the coast, though not south but north, to the state's northeast corridor with Edenton, Hertford, and Elizabeth City lined one after the other, towns not known for beaches but more for scenery, each with their own pretty rivers.

"Perquimans is an Indian name," Sid explained. "Perquimans means land of beautiful women." He smiled beneath his white mustache.

I kept returning to this sleepy sliver of the state because of the good stories and pretty pictures but also because I felt the rest of North Carolina had largely ignored it. I think even the area itself had a watery identity. Many people in that northeast corridor watched Virginia television. "WRAL?" they'd often ask with furrowed brows. "Oh, you're from Raleigh. What are you doing here?"

It was a two-and-a-half-hour drive from Raleigh to Hertford, more time than it would take me to drive from Hertford to my parents' house in Virginia Beach. I could understand why the area might feel more like an arm of Hampton Roads than a toe of the Tar Heel State.

But either way, Sid was unabashedly proud of his town, and I liked that. I also liked the way he said *town*. And *courthouse*. He emphasized the *ow* and the *ou*. "Let me show you around the courthouse in town."

The Perquimans County Courthouse is a Georgian-style structure, soft yellow with two white columns; a stately looking building. "There was actually a courthouse here before the town of Hertford," Sid said, and told me the first one was built in 1732 with the town soon following. "And the present courthouse goes back to 1825."

Sid led us inside, in and around the choppy layout, down narrow halls, up skinny staircases, and into small rooms. I met secretaries who smiled from cluttered desks. The courthouse appeared busy and apparently always had been, continuously for almost two hundred years. "From murder trials to probably somebody stealing a pig," Sid said.

It also served as a meeting place for the local Masonic lodge, and Sid had corralled the lodge leader to come sit for an interview. It must have been last minute—the man looked like a harried farmer who'd hustled over from the field. He was a little sweaty and unshaven and, rather strangely, wore an old-timey hat on his head, a black bowler, the kind my granddad would have worn to the office. I figured he must have frantically rooted through his attic and snatched the first respectable item within reach.

We were in an upstairs room with pictures of past Masonic chiefs circling the walls, many with beards hanging well beyond their chests—many with fancy fedoras, too. The current chief took a seat in a high-back chair, and it was a good look, the look of a throne with a small podium in front that conveniently hid his blue jeans. Draped over the podium was a silky blue banner with the word *Wisdom* stitched in gold.

He'd caught his breath by then, and I asked him how long the Masons had met in the courthouse. "Probably 150, 160 years," he said, and told me he was pretty sure his was the only Masonic lodge in the state that still met

in a public building. "The last one left in North Carolina." Then he sat forward in the high back, and it was truly an excellent look, the black hat not a bad substitute for a crown. The chief thrust out his chest. "It's one of the great fraternities in the world," he said with utmost authority.

I thanked him for the interview; I actually think by then he hated to see us go, but Sid hurried us along, back downstairs. He couldn't wait to show us more. He told me he'd saved the best for last.

He led me into one of the courthouse offices and pointed rather enthusiastically to a painting that hung over the mantel. It depicted two men. One looked rather aristocratic in a long coat and musketeer hat. The other man was wrapped in a shawl with a single feather in his hair. The two men seemed to be exchanging a handwritten sheet of paper.

Sid beamed and explained we were gazing upon a scene from 1662, when a white man paid an Indian chief for a piece of Perquimans County property. "And this is the first time we think the Indians were ever paid for their land." He gave me a minute to let that sink in. The white man had a long cruel history of stealing from Indians, but here was a legitimate business transaction, the aristocratic pilgrim paying the chief and acquiring land legally and respectfully.

Sid said it was believed to be the first transaction of its kind in North Carolina and perhaps anywhere in the country. "And we have the deed," he said and smiled as wide as the painting itself. Turned out, the painting was not the best-for-last. The deed was.

It was kept inside a vault, behind a thick metal door equipped with a combination dial. Sid spun it back and forth and twisted the vault's silver handle, and the door thunked open. I thought about asking him to close it and do it over again so we could capture more video and record another thunk. The door was fantastic, and I doubted the deed could beat it.

Sid handled the historic document with the tips of his fingers. His hands shook. "Here it is," he said. "First recorded land deed in North Carolina. We have the original. We have the oldest deed." The ink was surprisingly bold considering the document's age, but the words were written in cursive, and they were so swirly I couldn't read them. I figured whoever authored the deed must have had a flair for the dramatic. It didn't matter. The paper was enough.

"The oldest deed," Sid said. And beamed.

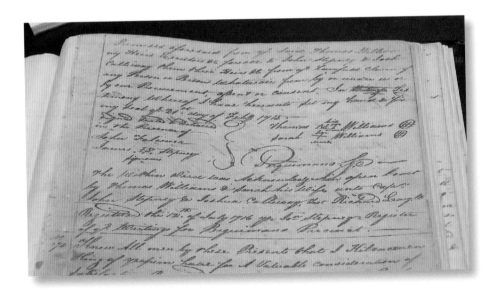

HERTFORD

THE MONUMENT

I remember the gnats.

They were everywhere—in my hair, my eyes, my mouth. Yuck! But at least I was behind the camera. The man I was interviewing couldn't talk without having a few fly in. I think he wanted to spit, but the best, most tasteful, thing he could do was to swat them away. Although swatting and speaking at the same time didn't make for such good television.

He was talking about the only monument of its kind in the state and one of the few of its kind in the country, a stone marker of enormous meaning. It wasn't especially tall; in fact, it was rather stubby as monuments go. The marker was an upright granite rectangle mounted atop a layered stone pedestal; the pedestal took up more than half the height. But the monument carried enormous historical weight, a Civil War stone that honored local blacks who had joined the Union. "These were soldiers from Perquimans County," said the gnat-eating Hertford mayor, a black man himself named Horace, who recited the stone's inscription: "In memory of the colored Union soldiers who fought in the war of 1861 to 1865."

It was a sweltering August day, another one of my trips to Hertford, and the gnats welcomed us in droves at the corner of Park and King. The monument stood at that intersection, between a light pole and stop sign and next to a rusty chain-link fence; part of the fence was badly bent and leaning, on the verge of collapsing. It was not a busy intersection, and the few drivers who pulled up obediently stopped to look for passing traffic—but probably not to look at the monument. It stood back from the curb, in its own lonesome corner, with nothing else around except for the light pole, stop sign, and collapsing fence.

I was pleased to see a brick church across the street, thinking the church lent a certain sanctity to the area; I felt the monument deserved some sanctity. But I couldn't help notice the houses nearby, sagging beneath the weight of despair; the houses seemed even heavier than the stone. "This is what we normally call the black neighborhood," Horace said with a couple of swats.

This was clearly the other side of the tracks, although there weren't any railroad tracks and no pretty Hertford water views, either. But the gnats didn't care. Black, white, rich, poor—the little devils loved on everybody.

"These were soldiers fighting for their cause," Horace said, admiring the stone, and I thought about that for a moment, their cause. They were local men, southern boys, who had crossed the line to fight for the North. Depending on how you looked at it, what they did was courageous and admirable or an atrocious act of betrayal. Either way, their side had won; the monument was a tribute to them and the cause they'd felt bound to uphold. And yet I found myself looking at the neighborhood and thinking *lost cause*, the term typically attached to the Confederacy.

"Do you wish the monument was in a more prominent place?" I asked Horace, not sure whether I should; I think he lived in the neighborhood, but I asked him anyway.

He thought a moment and shrugged. "I think it's okay."

He told me about the women who had erected it, black women of the United Daughters of Veterans who had rallied around the effort in the 1920s. They not only cobbled together the money and succeeded but made history in doing so. According to Horace, it was the only monument of its kind in the nation at the time it was built. "They wanted to recognize their people, and they had to pull together everything they had to do this, and I admire them for that."

I asked Horace if many people knew about the monument and whether it attracted tourists or even historians. He shrugged again and gazed at the stone. "Probably the only one in the South," he said. "This is part of our heritage, and we try to keep it up, keep it going."

He seemed like a humble man; he was rather soft-spoken, which I thought actually gave his words greater weight. The way he said what he said seemed important, and I was glad for that. His articulate sound bites would go nicely with video of the monument, would resonate with dramatic low-angle shots of the stone. We'd be able to cover most of Horace's interview and wouldn't need to show him much on camera. It would be better that way. We could avoid the gnats. We could spend more time honoring the men who fought for what they believed in.

HERTFORD

S BRIDGE

Sid drove us by Hertford's famous S bridge, and I was glad to see it still intact. I remembered the bridge from a few years before, during one of my first visits to town. Sid hadn't smiled much then. He was worried the state was going to tear it down because it was too old and costly to keep up.

It straddled the Perquimans River, but rather than a straight shot across, it curved in the shape of an S, not an I as in "immediate," the way most bridges are built, but S as in "swerve." Or "scenic" or "special." It was also short, just a few hundred yards long.

The bridge's midsection was metal with high sides and interlocking beams, a silver canopy tented over a narrow two-lane strip. Cars rumbled across but not fast. This was a bridge made for going slow, for admiring its old-timey quaintness and unusual curves and the quiet beauty outside the window.

Boats came and went, and the bridge opened and closed—and what a magnificent added feature that was. Down went the gates, stopping traffic, often to the delight of easy-going drivers who now had something else to marvel at: gears groaning to life, revolving wheels and greasy chains, the metal shuddering and bridge swiveling, expertly balanced on a solid center beam, pivoting and swinging wide.

Robert had so much fun zooming in on all the intricate workings that I think he wished for an armada of tall ships to sail up in fifteen-minute increments, enough time for the bridge to close before it had to quickly reopen. The Department of Transportation, on the other hand, probably wished the river allowed only dinghies.

The state favored scrapping the bridge because it broke down so often. It was built in 1928, and the mechanics were old and parts hard to come by. And yet Sid told me it was one of the last of its kind in the nation.

The bridge and causeway formed an S because the banks on either side weren't parallel to each other. "I've never been on any other bridge that

looks quite like it," said Hertford's planning director. Sid had gathered up all kinds of important people for me to interview.

"It's a historic monument," the town manager told me. "It's part of our town logo."

Indeed it was. I had remembered seeing it on the brochures in Sid's office.

"It's lovely. People come here just to see it," exclaimed a smiley woman with bouncy blonde hair; I think she smiled even more than Sid—except when talking about the bureaucrats in Raleigh; then her hair *really* bounced. "We would die," she said if the state replaced it with some modern-day concrete monstrosity. "There would be no town left." Though I think she meant to say no *tourists* left. I told her I'd talked with the suits and ties in Raleigh, the folks with the Department of Transportation, who'd said they were committed to designing the new bridge in the shape of an S, just like the current one. The woman shook her head. "If we make a loud enough noise, they will save *this* bridge."

I learned the S bridge had cost the state three million dollars in the past five years. "But I also look at what it costs to replace it," said the planning director. When I told him the state thought it would be cheaper in the long run, he hung his head. "I think they're pretty serious."

I drove across the bridge several times with Robert riding shotgun, his camera pointed out the window, aimed at the interlocking beams as we

passed, and beyond them the water sparkling in the sun. But it was the moon I thought of.

Hertford's S bridge was said to have inspired the song "Carolina Moon." The man who wrote it apparently penned it one moonlit night as he stood on the bridge overlooking the river. His name wasn't familiar to me, but some of the people who'd recorded it were, including Perry Como, Dean Martin, and Kate Smith.

I sang the song in my head while driving. Each trip across took only about thirty seconds, and I could barely finish a verse before I was making a U-turn and rumbling over the span again so Robert could capture more video. *Oh, Carolina Moon keep shining, shining on the one who waits for me, Carolina Moon I'm pining, pining for the place I long to be.*

The moon sounded rather majestic in the song and when I pictured it gleaming over the water. But the words also spoke of longing and heartache, which today seemed poignantly appropriate.

Although I wasn't thinking of the future just then. No, I was content merely singing the tune and enjoying the ride, appreciating the S and the beautiful view outside the window.

POSTSCRIPT

As of this writing, the North Carolina Department of Transportation plans to replace the original S bridge, with construction set to begin in the spring of 2019.

Oh, Carolina Moon keep shining . . .

The plan is to construct the new bridge also in the shape of an S.

I'm pining, pining for the place I long to be . . .

HERTFORD

THE TURTLE LOG

The S bridge was within sight of the turtle log. I had reached the end of my list. The turtle log at last.

"Turtles are always here," Sid said. We had returned to the banks of the Perquimans, and the turtles didn't disappoint. They sunned, they crawled, they shoved, they plopped. Sid told me the log had been in place for more than a hundred years.

"Wow," I said. "Do you remember it as a kid?"

"Remember it? That's how I learned to count!"

He said he used to peer out the window of the family car, and his mom would ask how many turtles he saw. "And I'd say three or I'd say five." I took another look at the log and thought five turtles bunched together on it would have been an awfully tight squeeze. Forget about learning to count to six.

"We have our bridge, our charter date of 1758, and the turtle log," Sid said and told me the town's seal included all three. "They're all very important to us."

We stood on the banks for a good long while, sunning ourselves, too, and I couldn't help but wonder what other reporters would think of me spending so much time on a story about a log, even if it did have turtles on it. "This lets you slow down," Sid said, emphasizing the *ow* in d*ow*n. "Just slow down and enjoy life." He smiled beneath his white mustache.

His words drifted through my head as we rolled back through town, and as we did, I noticed turtles everywhere, decorative ones in store windows and even painted on the sidewalk. Hertford was a turtle town, and I grinned at the thought. And at another thought.

I thought about those other reporters, busy chasing news, and wondered if they'd ever set foot in Hertford. I doubted they had. They wouldn't have had the time. I bet they weren't slowing down at all. Too bad for them.

Maybe at times we all need to move at a turtle's pace.

ANSON COUNTY

THE FIRST, THE EPICENTER, AND THE OUTLAW

First things first.

It was 2012, five years since the Tar Heel Traveler debuted on WRAL, and I sat at my desk with a well-worn state map splayed out over everywhere. My pen and pad were buried somewhere underneath the map, and I lifted and rummaged gently because I'd taped the creases, and the last thing the map needed was another tear. I supposed I could have bought a new map, but I tend to get attached to things.

When I was finally settled and studying the blue landscape before me, wondering where to go next, it dawned on me that Robert and I had traveled to almost every jagged square of North Carolina; we'd traversed so many of those dotted red lines to shoot stories, block by block, one county after another.

I had done a sloppy taping job—some of the squares representing counties were miserably askew—but the state itself had a sensible symmetry. North Carolina comprised an even one hundred counties.

I traced my finger from coast to mountains. "Been there, been there . . ." I murmured while at the same time keeping a running tally. My pad was quickly filling with slash marks; each slash I made was a county I had visited. By the time I reached Cherokee at my map's tattered edge, I was at ninety-five slashes and on my second sheet of paper.

I realized I had just five counties to go before I could proudly say I'd covered stories in all one hundred. I hadn't set out to visit them all; it just happened that my stories had thus far taken me to ninety-five. And now I was in year five of the Tar Heel Traveler series, and it seemed only right to visit the final five before year five turned to year six. I liked the idea—and the symmetry of it, too.

I smoothed the wrinkles and tapped my finger on a dark-green blotch. Four of the remaining counties were in the mountains, which was a long haul with some miserably twisty roads. I knew sooner or later I'd have to suffer that drive if I was to accomplish my goal. But first . . .

I set my eyes on another unfamiliar county, much closer and easier to get to and one that practically begged for the ninety-sixth slash mark. It wasn't even that far from Charlotte, just a little east and south, tucked at the map's bottom edge near the South Carolina line. I studied the block letters in the blue square; in fact, I even reached for my reading glasses to make sure I had the name right—the letters were hazy beneath the tape.

I smiled when the county name in all caps came into clearer view. In fact, I even stamped my index finger in the space between the dotted lines.

Next stop: Anson County.

ANSON COUNTY

LILESVILLE

We arrived late afternoon and didn't have much light left, but that's what happens when you shoot several stories in one day. When you finally reach the last one, you're usually fighting the dark. We were also fighting the drizzle.

Ours was a dreary welcome to Anson County, Anson being the whole reason for the trip, but it was hard to pass by other stories while passing through other counties. So we were late arriving, which was all backward. Our last shoot should have been first. Definitely first.

We pulled into Lilesville, population five hundred or so. I'd learned of the town when researching the county. The county wasn't big, either, but I figured there had to be a story we could do; *any* story would do, any story in Anson that would get us another county closer to conquering all one hundred.

Lilesville was quiet and the wipers lazy as they intermittently swept raindrops from our windshield. I figured a person who didn't know Lilesville would no doubt drive right on through. There wasn't even a stoplight to stop them, not a single stoplight in town.

And yet Lilesville was a town of firsts. It proudly claimed the first all-fireproof building in America. "Well, that's the Lilesville School," said Juanita, the former longtime town clerk. I interviewed her in a conference room at the town hall. She had only recently retired and yet looked as though she still belonged at the office, or maybe that was just because of the television interview. She wore a black dress and pearl earrings, and her red lipstick matched the color of her sweater. She told me the school was built and fireproofed in 1923. "It was the materials that the building was made from."

She showed me the town banner with the school printed on it. It was a big, solid-looking building in the shape of a rectangle, topped with a cupola. Juanita said it was also the first school in North Carolina to serve hot lunches.

"Two firsts?"

She nodded and told me about the teacher named Miss Betty who cooked the lunches herself. "Vegetable soup from home and brought it to her students."

Juanita mentioned other firsts. Lilesville was the first town to have a phone system, she said. But it wasn't the first in the state, only the county, which to me seemed like a "smaller" first.

"Also, the first black female mayor," she said. That was another county first, although one that sounded like a much bigger first.

The conference room we sat in was full of windows, and I could see daylight fading fast between the blinds. It also looked like the rain had let up. We needed video around town, and I asked Juanita if she'd mind giving us a tour.

Our first stop was the bank, just an ordinary brick block of a building. She told me it was the first bank in Anson County to have a drive-through window. It also seemed aptly named: First National.

She drove us to a pretty house tucked at the end of a long driveway. The driveway itself was impressive, lined with trees whose intertwining limbs formed a dense canopy. The house was a large two-story, painted white with tall columns and an elegant front porch, which may sound like a contradiction—an elegant porch?—but this one really was. The dark floorboards and rocking chairs gleamed, as if the painter had just left. Candles glowed from the lower windows, and the shrubs in front were lush and full. A decorative flag waved. The wind was steady.

Juanita had called the mayor of Lilesville, and he met us at the front of the drive; he was a round-faced man in his sixties who wore a windbreaker and wide-brimmed canvas hat.

"Imported sandstone brick from England," he said of the house and told me it was the first of its kind anywhere around, not just in Anson County but beyond. Not only that, he said, but the homeowner claimed a first, too. "She started one of the first garden clubs in the county." I admired the shrubs again and nodded.

"We're the best kept secret in North Carolina," the mayor said. I asked him if the town might get a stoplight one day. "Maybe we will, but I don't think in my lifetime," he said and laughed.

There was still more town to see, and we continued the tour with Juanita. She showed us another house, completely different from what we'd just seen. It was old, abandoned, and suffering from a bad case of peeling paint. "Invaded by Sherman's army in 1865," Juanita said.

I could see how the place might have been handsome in its prime. It was a towering house, large for its time, and one that had apparently been well furnished, which suited Sherman's army. "They opened the baby grand piano and poured horse feed in; the horses ate out of the piano."

I told Juanita that definitely had to be a first, and she smiled.

There was another house to see, she said, a little ways out of town. She glanced at the gray sky and asked if we wouldn't mind going ahead without

her. She was sure we'd want pictures once we heard the background. She told me the story quickly. "Another first," she said with a second glance at the swollen sky. "But you better hurry."

We followed her directions, drove along narrow roads, and at last came to a sad little house on a hill. It was a vast sweeping hill, and we parked on the street with the house in the distance. It was a lonely look but a scenic one, too—which is probably why Steven Spielberg picked it.

This was where Spielberg filmed key scenes of his 1985 movie *The Color Purple*. "Of course, we were so excited," Juanita had told me earlier. When I asked why the filmmakers had picked Lilesville, she said, simply, "Well, it's a nice place to make a movie."

I watched the movie when I returned to Raleigh, and when we eventually edited our Lilesville story, we dissolved back and forth between the film scenes and the video we'd shot that gloomy afternoon. It was a big difference. In the movie, young girls skip through a field of glorious purple flowers that are chest high and waving in the breeze. I'd heard Spielberg ordered all those flowers brought in and planted.

Our video, on the other hand, showed a lonesome house atop a barren hill, and I wondered if that's also what Spielberg had seen when he first pulled up. If so, I had to compliment him on his vision. He'd turned a nondescript landscape into one of movie history's signature settings. One critic praised *The Color Purple*'s strong sense of place and said it was comparable to Oz or Tara in *Gone with the Wind*. I had to agree. It was so strong that when

I looked at our gloomy video, I couldn't help but see those glorious flowers and the happy girls on screen playing patty-cake in the field.

"You know, we have a saying down here that a day out of Lilesville is a day wasted," Juanita had said. "We're proud of Lilesville," and I could tell she meant it. In fact, I found she had helped alter my own view—and I guess Steven Spielberg had, too.

It was easy to underestimate such a small town in such a sleepy county. I had at first, until I learned of its firsts. Now I would never look at Lilesville the same way. I would instead think of purple flowers and green shrubs, a piano trough and bank drive-through. I'd remember the nice-looking school on the town banner and think of Miss Betty's hot vegetable soup. I found I admired this little town of firsts.

Only when we rolled out of town did the downpour begin, and I felt it was as if the weather had waited for us, as if Mother Nature had been supremely patient on our behalf. She had held back the rain and politely allowed us to shoot our story—first.

ANSON COUNTY

SOLAR ECLIPSE

We eventually did conquer all one hundred counties.

In fact, we even returned to Anson County a few times. One time we stayed in Wadesboro, which is not much bigger than Lilesville, and yet it's the county seat. Robert and I grabbed two rooms at the local motel. There weren't many restaurants to choose from, so we ate at our old reliable: Waffle House, both dinner at night and breakfast the next morning. Good cheese eggs and coffee.

At the time, we were shooting a piece on an old store known for its delicious cuts of meat. The store owner was also the butcher, a nice man who threw scraps to the dogs. And that's what I remember most, not the paying customers at the counter but the wagging tails outside the door.

It was during that trip when somebody mentioned a major event that had happened in Wadesboro, and the more the person talked, the more I had a feeling I'd be visiting the motel and Waffle House again in the future.

So we returned, this time in May 2016—because of May 1900. Back then, Wadesboro had captured global attention. "Wadesboro, North Carolina, little Anson County, was ground zero," Tommy Allen said.

Tommy had been the longtime sheriff, though he'd recently retired. He volunteered at the historical society and arrived in his pickup to let us in. I was impressed to see the society had a building all its own, one filled with historical files and photos.

Tommy was a shorter man with glasses. He wore a collared shirt and jeans and said he was enjoying retirement; he could entertain his interest in history and wear what he wanted.

"It was May the 28th, 1900," he said, seated at a long table with folders open in front of him. "The press came down here from all over the world." He plucked out a picture and slid it toward me. I examined what looked to be a group of reporters, some holding cameras. Each man wore either a bow tie or string tie, which they hadn't loosened despite the springtime heat. Although the air was about to turn much cooler, for they were at the epicenter of the 1900 solar eclipse.

"One hundred miles in either direction, you saw only a partial eclipse," Tommy said. "But Wadesboro was the total eclipse. Right here." He handed me other pictures to prove it. Several showed an enormous black ball edged with a radiant glow. "They were studying the corona," he said and traced his finger along the edge of the circle. "The corona around the sun, that little glow when it's a perfect eclipse."

The images seemed especially dramatic for the time period; those 1900 cameras had done an admirable job. The cameras were monsters. I gaped at one photo that showed a young man posing by one that looked like a cannon and wondered how he'd been able to mount it on the tripod. And yet the fella's bow tie was in place—although he had rolled his shirt sleeves to his elbows.

"The Smithsonian sent two train-car loads of equipment down here," Tommy said, shuffling through more pictures. "Here's a group from the naval observatory." Astronomers had apparently spent weeks in Wadesboro preparing for the big day. "Scientists from everywhere. Some of them had moons and planets named after them."

They were famous but also friendly. Tommy said one of the astronomers even joined the local church choir to sing on Sundays.

And then came May 28th.

"They were taking thousands of pictures," he said and flipped again to the money shots, the moon blotting the sun, which I found both eerie and awe inspiring. The astronomers had brought their own monster cameras, which had expertly captured that rare peculiarity of nature.

Tommy must have seen how awestruck I was and told me about the planetarium in town, probably thinking I might like to see it, that it might add to my story. I'd actually learned of it when researching Wadesboro and had been surprised; I thought planetariums were mainly found in big cities and university towns.

Tommy shut off the lights and locked the building, and we followed him to a nearby school, site of the planetarium. He introduced me to Wendy who looked like a scientist herself, which I supposed she was. Her glasses were thick and large and the moon looming over her gray and pockmarked. She'd projected it on the domed ceiling. "Wow," I said. The interview setting was spectacular—I imagined the reporters from 1900 being both amazed and envious.

"They did a huge amount of study," she said of those long-ago astronomers. "They checked the cloud cover for three years to find the optimal viewing place, and believe it or not, Wadesboro, North Carolina, was pretty much the optimal viewing place."

I listened but had a hard time taking my eyes off the moon rotating on the ceiling. It continually moved, grew large and small and large again.

"It was right here," Wendy said. "The total solar eclipse where the moon passes totally in front of the sun."

I had seen a partial eclipse once as a kid growing up in Massachusetts and remembered grownups warning my friend Jimmy and me not to look at the sun—but of course we did, stealing a few quick glances. And then the sun was gone, most of it anyway, and the day instantly turned dark and cool. But only for a minute. And yet that minute had left a lasting impression.

"The roosters were crowing and everything else," Wendy said. I figured there were probably quite a few roosters in Wadesboro in 1900. "You know, they were feeling like it was nighttime."

"Was it a successful viewing?" I asked, although I was pretty sure I knew the answer, having seen those dramatic eclipse pictures back at the historical society.

"It was a very successful viewing," Wendy said.

We commiserated a bit about the eclipse's aftermath, when reporters packed up and all the famous scientists left town and when the church choir had one less member. The outsiders had become part of the community, if only for a short time, and they had left a lasting impression, too—or at least that was Wendy's impression. She was sure they must have departed with a great sense of satisfaction, for they had documented one of the rare mysteries of the universe and in doing so had perhaps gained a bit more knowledge.

"And maybe they learned something else," I said. "Maybe they learned that Wadesboro is a pretty good little town?"

"I hope so," she said and smiled.

And the moon revolved.

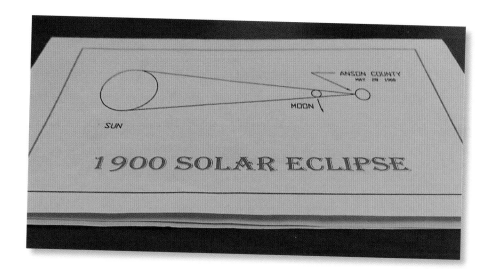

ANSON COUNTY

THE OUTLAW

What a strange name it was. Tommy Allen had to spell it for me.

The retired sheriff from Anson County who'd patiently waited on me at the planetarium thought I might be interested in one more nugget before leaving town. He said it was one that had always interested *him*, a cops-and-robbers, shoot-'em-up kind of story. "Definitely," I said.

He began by spelling the unusual name. "M-O-M-E," he said. And then, "D-I-G-G-S." He told me Mome Diggs had robbed banks and stage-coaches and was once part of the notorious James Gang. He had ridden with Jesse James.

"*The* Jesse James?" I asked.

Tommy nodded and told me Mome had been from Anson County and asked if I'd like to see his grave.

Robert and I followed him to the county's western edge, to a little community called Peachland. Pine View Cemetery was a quiet sweep of land dotted with headstones just off the highway. I doubted passersby even gave it a look.

We parked near the gate and humped up the hill to an old stone, waist high and spotted black with mold. *A. Mome,* it read, and Tommy explained the A stood for Andrew and that "Mome" had been his nickname. Engraved at the bottom were the dates 1857 and 1897. "Forty years old," I said. "I'm surprised he lived that long."

I'd seen plenty of old cowboy flicks and knew a fella could get shot just by looking at somebody the wrong way—at least in the movies. Although this was rural Anson County, and if it was sleepy now, I figured it must have been dead back then. "How did he hook up with Jesse James?" I asked.

Tommy began by telling me about another outlaw from the next county over: Merriman Little, who had been running with the James Gang. Merriman was the one who'd recruited Mome to come along. "He

and Merriman would leave for a time and do their robberies and then come back here and stay."

I took a moment to take in the immediate area. Thick woods bordered the cemetery. I didn't see a building in sight and heard only the distant highway; the faint whoosh of passing cars sounded more like a gentle breeze. Tommy said Jesse James himself occasionally hid out in Peachland. "That's the word."

He handed me a newsletter from the historical society; he'd brought one along and pointed to a Rhett Butler–looking fellow peering from the front page. The name below the picture was Mome Diggs, and the name above it? Tommy Allen. I scanned Tommy's latest byline.

I read that Jesse James had caught the bullet that killed him in 1882, which meant Mome was abruptly out of a job. So he had come back home to quiet Peachland, which might have been a tad too quiet because one day he saddled up and rode toward the big town of Charlotte. "And he ended up in some sort of brawl outside a bar in Monroe and was killed," Tommy said.

For years Mome had run from the law and dodged flying bullets, and in the end a little barroom brawl did him in. Maybe now he was at peace, I thought, and studied the tombstone. I was especially struck by an image of clasped hands carved at the top, and wondered at their meaning.

Perhaps it was symbolic: Mome shaking hands with his savior—or his mentor, Jesse James.

"I was sheriff of Anson County for twenty-eight years," Tommy said. "Yeah, Mome Diggs would have gone to jail if I'd known about him."

Poor Mome, I thought. I couldn't help it, despite all the bad he had done. He had been largely forgotten, not to mention overshadowed by Jesse James. All that was left was Mome's moldy grave—and of course, Tommy's newsletter and my soon-to-be Tar Heel Traveler story. And so maybe Mome wasn't so forgotten after all.

"Yeah, he would have gone to jail," Tommy repeated, and at that moment the carving of those clasped hands seemed to come alive for me. I imagined one of the hands being Tommy's, ready to slap the cuffs on that other hand—Mome's.

MURPHY

MANHUNT

In my mind, Murphy has always had a kind of eerie, spooky, unsettling mystique about it. Maybe because it's so far out there, 360 miles west of Raleigh. That's a six-hour car ride, or seven because of the mountain roads—seven-and-a-half with bathroom breaks.

Murphy is at the edge of the Great Smokies, beyond the Nantahala Gorge, in Cherokee County, home to the Hiawasee River that runs through town. Cherokee, Nantahala, Hiawasee—the names themselves possess an eerie mystique.

"Welcome to Raleigh. We're sending you to Murphy." That's about how it went when WRAL hired me in 1997. I was the station's new documentary producer and— "Hey," said the station's head honchos, "there's a serial bomber on the loose near Murphy. That'd be a good one. Our next doc."

The fugitive's name was Eric Rudolph, "the Abortion Clinic Bomber," who also targeted the 1996 Olympics in Atlanta, killing one and wounding more than a hundred others. Rudolph had spent his teenage years in western North Carolina, and that's where agents tracked him after Atlanta. They were sure he was hunkered down in the thick woods and hollows of Cherokee County. He was a survivalist after all, able to live off the land without man-made shelter or supermarket groceries. Rudolph's reputation became almost mythological, to the point of folk-hero status. Some were actually rooting for him—and wagering on him. How long could he avoid capture? Years began to seem like a safe bet when day after day weary agents emerged from the woods and tromped back to their hotel rooms, boots caked with mud, trousers pricked from thorns. All they managed to catch were ticks.

It was one of the largest manhunts in US history and, ooh, that was mighty juicy. "And it's in our backyard!" the honchos exclaimed. The "backyard" was a hard day's drive, harder when we hit the mountains. The roads curved and the foliage closed in, and the claustrophobia turned creepier the deeper we went; the sun ran away, and the walls reached out: rocky, jagged, threatening.

A photographer and I must have made that trip ten times, always going back for more, for a news conference or reported sighting or for more interviews. Naturally, I kept looking out the car window, eyes peeled for Rudolph. I wouldn't have minded being the hero. I could see the headline: REPORTER NABS KILLER! Instead, I nearly wound up a casualty.

There was a whole radical, skin-head, white nationalist, antigovernment vibe simmering in that dark, dense wilderness, and it was all tangled up in the hunt for Eric Rudolph, the bomber himself a militant antigay, antiabortion extremist. The honchos thought that was juicy, too, and said we had to include that angle in the doc.

I found myself one day—a day I dearly hoped was not the last of my life—sitting on a couch, facing an elder skin head; in fact, he was *the* head, the supreme leader of the western North Carolina government-conspiracy movement. Thankfully, I was not alone. There was the photographer I worked with, and we'd brought an anchorman with us whom the station had picked to "front" the documentary. He'd come nicely dressed in suit and tie and took a seat on an opposite couch.

I hated to even think it, but I figured Mr. Anchorman would be Mr. Skin Head's first target should the conversation turn ugly. Me? I was just the lowly producer. And yet I'd managed to track this maniacal militant; I'd actually found his phone number and called him up. "Ahhh, uhmm . . . ," is how I'd begun, stammering all over myself on the phone. But somehow I had talked myself into his house—with a camera, too.

But he wouldn't allow us to turn the camera on yet. First, some preliminary matters. He wanted to discuss his views so we knew where he stood before rolling. "Briefly," he said.

For three hours we sat listening to him vent against the government, the president, the CIA, FBI, and everyone else in authority. He ranted and raved and pulled books off the shelf and jabbed a finger at fine print, which he claimed was proof—PROOF!—that the United States had lied, cheated, stolen, robbed, beaten, betrayed. "Not gonna take it anymore!" he cried, spittle flying from cracked lips. Meanwhile, a young cohort of his—perhaps his son or nephew or merely some high school apprentice—sat on a third couch, eyes dead, hands folded, unmoving, unblinking the entire time. Then again, I myself never uttered a sound, and neither did the photographer. The anchorman kept his words to a minimum—I must say, he was a savvy anchor; our ratings were quite good.

Finally—three brutal hours later—the brutal one himself, Mr. Skin Head, with veins popping from his head, slowly swiveled his beet-red face and stared each of us dead in the eyes, one by one by one. You could have heard a pin drop. Or a bullet drop into a chamber. Or a bowie knife slip from a sheath. The moment hung; the tension peaked. "Nah," he said at last, and the supreme skin head shook his skinned head. "Not gonna go on camera, but thank ya' for coming."

I should have been devastated by losing the interview—losing all that time—but when I stepped out of his house, I took a quick second to gaze at the sky, breathe deep, and send up a thank-you. Then we jumped in the car and skedaddled out of there.

I found out later Mr. Skin Head went to prison shortly after our visit. The government nabbed him for tax evasion.

Our documentary aired in 1999 with Rudolph still on the run. I often thought of those poor, weary, muddy, thorn-pricked federal agents. Most stayed at the little hotel in Andrews, the town next to Murphy, and the accommodations weren't so bad. I had stayed at the same hotel while shooting the doc and had been glad for the Huddle House right next door. I like Huddle House and could eat bacon and eggs every day, but I'm not sure I could every day for half a decade.

The long hunt for Rudolph didn't end until 2003. A rookie policeman found him rummaging through a dumpster at four in the morning and arrested him, and soon the baby-faced rookie officer became a nationwide hero.

The agents, on the other hand, were never in on the arrest. They might have been eating bacon and eggs at Huddle House that early morning. Or spraying themselves with tick repellent.

So, I was headed back to Cherokee County. It was 2016, and my documentary days had long since ended. I had returned to my roots, the way I'd begun my career, as a reporter broadcasting in front of the camera, though now I was the short-sleeved, laid-back Tar Heel Traveler.

I peered out the window on the way. No serial bomber, no skin head, no worries. But I still couldn't believe I was willingly headed Back-to-the-Beyond—I looked out the window to keep from getting car sick. The curves became curvier and the canopy heavier the deeper we drove.

But a good story surpasses all, and I was sure one awaited me at the end of the road. I had recently read about an odd icon on a Murphy hilltop. It was something normally found not in the cool claustrophobic mountains but in the sweltering wide-open desert.

Murphy was home to the Murphy Pyramid.

MURPHY

THE MURPHY PYRAMID

The ride was rugged but the town scenic.

I bet other towns would love to claim its courthouse for their own—lift it, set it on a flatbed, and move it. Except that would take the work of an army of Greek gods.

The Cherokee County Courthouse is enormous, impressive, and solid, like something the Greek gods might have found in Rome, although it's not close to ancient. Built in 1926, partly from blue marble quarried nearby, the courthouse stands two stories tall but looks far taller. It shoots directly skyward and is topped with a domed cupola inlaid with a working clock. The courthouse is a focal point, rising from the corner of Central and Peachtree Streets and proudly listed on the National Register of Historic Places.

But Murphy is also small and quaint. Someday I'd like to do a story on its 1934 movie theater, which survived the Great Depression when so many other theaters did not. It's a little red-and-white building with a big hen painted in the middle of the marquee. The Henn takes its name from its founder, and I'm glad he didn't resist the play on words and fluffy imagery.

Seventeen hundred people live in Murphy, and I'm sure they enjoy its tree-lined streets, shops, and restaurants. And what an affable mayor, maybe the friendliest, most outgoing mayor I've ever met.

Bill Hughes loves talking about Murphy. "A mountain treasure," he called it, among many other descriptive adjectives. And now a television crew from Raleigh was here? Well, that was like offering icing to a cake lover. What a marvelous chance to promote North Carolina's jewel of the west—"jewel" was one of his descriptors, too.

"So you want to see the pyramid?" he said, though perhaps a bit reluctantly. I think he would have preferred showing us the courthouse. But he took us to the hilltop, and there it stood, a perfect triangle made of stone—it was also shaped like a teepee; we were, after all, in the land of the Cherokee. "It's twenty-five-feet high, built around 1930," Bill said. "Beautiful location."

From the hill I could see most of Murphy in the near distance and the swirling Hiawassee directly below. My overlook provided a magnificent view, and I was surprised I hadn't been joined by any other sightseers, but Bill explained we were on private property. I assumed he'd made a phone call, or maybe the mayor didn't need approval. He looked rather official: crisp white shirt, red-striped tie, buttoned blue blazer, and a Murphy insignia pinned to his lapel. His wavy white hair and tinted sunglasses gave him a distinguished Hollywood look. And as it turned out, the story came with a California angle.

He began by telling me about Lillie Hitchcock Coit, born 1843, died 1929. "She was a unique individual," Bill said. He explained that she'd lived in San Francisco but had loved to travel and was so impressed by the pyramids of Egypt that she had one of her own built in Murphy. She built it in honor of her grandparents, who died in the mid-1800s and who'd been pioneers, the first white settlers to migrate to Murphy. Their names were

engraved in the center of the pyramid, along with an inscription in capital letters that read Sacred to the Memory. "Her grandparents and a niece are believed to be entombed underneath," explained Bill.

I turned when I heard the word *entombed* and thought, *What?* Bill's face suddenly seemed pinched. He told me, in rather somber fashion, that Lillie Coit had had their bodies exhumed from their original resting place and moved to the quiet hilltop. Soon after, she ordered construction of the pyramid.

I think my face had become pinched, too—from trying not to smile given the grave subject matter. My story had just gained an unexpected layer, and stories with surprises are the best kind. But the surprises didn't end there. I also learned Coit possessed a few layers of her own.

In pictures I saw later, she always wore long dresses with multiple folds, buttoned all the way to her neck. The dresses looked nearly as heavy as the pyramid, although she obviously wasn't one to be weighed down by formality. One photo showed her puffing a fat cigar and grinning. "She loved to smoke cigars," Bill said. "She was a crack shot with a rifle." I also read she was such an avid gambler that she often ditched the dresses and disguised herself as a man so she could gamble in male-only establishments.

She had an even greater fascination with firefighting that began as a teenager when she witnessed a shorthanded engine company respond to a call and pitched in to help. After that, the grateful firefighters made her an honorary member of the squad, and she routinely joined the team on the truck, racing to fires and riding in parades. In one picture, she wore a ridiculously tall fireman's hat in the shape of a triangle.

I suspected she would have been proud of the pyramid, and I felt sorry she didn't get to see it. She died before its completion.

"Beautiful location," Bill said again, and it was, especially now in the spring. From where we stood, I could see the great marble courthouse framed by dogwoods in the foreground, their branches full and feathery white. The river gently swished, and the sound was peaceful and soothing. "She just found it to be a suitable spot for the resting place of her grandparents."

I supposed the ground really was sacred, knowing that Lillie Coit's memorial was also a gravestone. I gazed up and admired what she had built and had no need to shade my eyes, for the pyramid cast a long shadow.

Far longer than I could ever have imagined.

"In the 1830s, Fort Butler was constructed on this site," Bill said and gestured at the open land. "The soldiers were brought in to round up the Cherokee and take them to Oklahoma, which led to the infamous Trail of Tears." I stiffened at his mention of the trail, for I knew about its torturous history, the forced relocation of Native Americans. As many as eight thousand Cherokee men, women, and children died along the trail, many from starvation.

My pyramid piece was suddenly taking a new direction. Bill pointed to the ground. "The trail began here with Fort Butler," he said. "Right here. This was the beginning."

I learned Fort Butler had included barracks, offices, shops, and other buildings, all sprawled across this very hill. The fort was a US Army headquarters, the unit charged with forcing Cherokee off their land, which would have been a monumental task. Once again, I thought of the names I'd encountered on my long trip to Murphy: Nantahala Gorge, Hiawassee River, Cherokee County. The Cherokee had been embedded in this region—their legacy still is—but during the summer of 1838, soldiers had been bent on removing them. They rounded up thousands of Cherokee and imprisoned them at Fort Butler before sending them to other internment camps and finally onto the Trail of Tears, where so many suffered horrible deaths. "The trail began here," Bill repeated, and I was struck by the reality of what he was saying, the immediacy of it. "Right here."

"Do you think Lillie Coit knew that?" I asked.

"I feel sure she probably did."

I felt sure, too. She seemed a woman ahead of her time. I read she occasionally wore pants when few women dared do something so outlandish back then. She'd probably been considered an outcast, but I was happy for Lillie—happy she was able to find some relief from those heavy dresses.

"Lillie Hitchcock *Coit*," Bill said. "You've heard of the Coit Tower?" I had but was startled at the connection.

"You mean . . . ," I started to ask. He nodded and told me the iconic Coit Tower in San Francisco was her idea. "You can go into the tower and see the entire city of San Francisco."

Coit Tower is a 210-foot cylinder, topped with an observation deck. Some say it looks like a fire hose with a nozzle at the end. I was sure Lillie would have been pleased with it, but she never saw the completion of that landmark, either. It was built in 1933 with money she had left behind for civic beautification.

"She must have been wealthy," I said, and Bill nodded.

"In San Francisco society, she ranked very high."

I wondered about the people who climbed Coit Tower every day, whether any of them knew the story of Lillie Coit. Or if many people in Murphy even knew about the existence of the Murphy Pyramid. "The reason there's so little known about it locally is because it's not open to the public," Bill said. "And you can understand why."

The why, I supposed, was because of the bodies buried beneath the pyramid. And because of the cruel treatment of the Cherokee, although from where I stood, there was no trace of that sad history, only a grassy hill and a lonely pyramid.

"I think it's one of the most unusual structures in the state," Bill said, and we both admired it. Twenty-five feet was not overly tall, a fraction of the size of an Egyptian pyramid, and yet this time I did shelter my eyes, for the sun had settled directly above it, in line with the pyramid's point. The sight was not only beautiful but powerful.

"I think it's fascinating," Bill said and paused before repeating himself. "I think it's fascinating."

I lowered my sheltered eyes, which came to rest upon the word *Sacred*.

MURPHY

THE MOON-EYED PEOPLE

"This is where the Moon-Eyed People were found," said Wanda Stalcup, and I waited for her to laugh. She didn't. Although she did smile.

Wanda was, at the time, the pleasant director of the Cherokee County Historical Museum in downtown Murphy. I enjoyed the museum, my kind of place, very library-ish, a bit dark and leathery, loaded with old books and ancient people peering from the walls, and so many crusty artifacts.

Wanda fit the place perfectly. She was librarian-ish, neatly dressed, her black-and-gray hair cut short, little round glasses perched on her nose. She flitted from one part of the room to the next, telling me about all the local history; the area was a historical hotbed because of the rich Cherokee heritage.

When she mentioned the Moon-Eyed People, I thought she was kidding, but I was the only one who laughed. She began to tell me the story, and it was the first subject she didn't flit from, except when she brought up fairies and talked of fairy crosses. She was losing me, although she seemed to be connecting the fairies with . . . *Moon-Eyed People?* I thought. I could just see my news director now, his eyes as big as moons rolling in disgust at such nonsense.

I tried to stay with Wanda's story. I nodded as she talked and liked her quiet enthusiasm. She seemed shy but well-informed and level-headed. *Level-headed?* I heard my news director harrumph in my head. But, yes, she was very down to earth. She was talking about Moon-Eyed People without so much as a snicker. But my news director was both snickering and scoffing in my ear. I had a tough time concentrating. "Let me show you something," Wanda said at last, perhaps reacting to my blank face. What she showed me was a blank face. Two of them.

It was a three-foot-high stone carving of aliens—or at least that's what they looked like to me—two little armless aliens from outer space joined at the sides like Siamese twins. They were propped in a large case and seemed to peer rather sadly from behind the glass, which I knew didn't make sense because they had no eyeballs with which to peer. They had only shallow divots for eyes, and no expressions to indicate sadness, just plain round faces, very flat, with simple noses and short slash marks for mouths. Somebody had placed a chain around them, covered in leather, and attached it to the back of the case to keep them from falling, and I also found that sad, as though they were tied against their will and locked up, those strange space aliens. But, of course, none of this was real. *Was it?*

"Who made it, I don't know," Wanda said and told me the figures were made of soapstone. "And they were pecked not carved."

"What do you mean pecked?" I said. "Pecked, like with a stone?"

She nodded. "Pecked with a stone, with a harder stone."

I thought about that for a moment, in part because of the way she answered, how she nodded—slowly, knowingly. Her lips had tightened, and her eyes had grown wider. Or maybe I was simply groping for facial expressions that weren't there at all.

"Pecked," I said. "Without tools. So that makes you think they were made long ago?"

"That's correct," she said and allowed a smile, like a wise teacher who's just led her floundering pupil to the right answer. And maybe the smile was also a way to soften the strangeness of what came next.

According to legend, Wanda said, a group of little people lived in Cherokee County hundreds of years ago. "They were very small people with flat faces, light skin, and blue eyes, and they were blinded by sunlight, so they only came out at night. They lived in mounds and caves and in the woods, according to legend." She seemed careful to include attribution. "According to legend, they were round-faced like the moon, and that's how they obtained the name Moon-Eyed People."

The Siamese twins behind the glass did have round faces, but they weren't identical twins. One was a few inches taller than the other and bigger all around. A father and son, or mother and daughter maybe? Wanda shrugged when I asked and said there had been many theories. She told me a local farmer had found the statue in 1842 when he was clearing his land. By then, the Moon-Eyed People had long since disappeared, Wanda said—according to legend.

The farmer wasn't sure what he'd found. It was heavy, about three hundred pounds. He dragged it to his well house, propped it against the side, and left it there, outside, for years. Eventually, somebody else ended up with the effigy—"effigy" is what Wanda sometimes called the statue. For years it was lost, and then for a time it stood outside of a motel in Macon County. It changed hands, and in 2015 the Cherokee County Historical Museum managed to acquire it.

Wanda offered me another pleasant smile and told me she had something else to show me. We walked across the room, past cases full of arrowheads, and came to a display of curious-looking stones, each small enough to fit in the palm of a hand. They were generally dark in color and all shaped like crosses.

"Fairy crosses," Wanda said. "According to legend, when Christ was crucified, the Little People cried, and the tears that hit the ground are actually what formed the fairy crosses.

They were formed from their tears. But they haven't been carved; it's a natural formation."

I took a closer look. Some of the crosses were cruder than others, and each of their cross "beams" were short, although there was no doubt they formed a cross shape. There were dozens on display, perhaps hundreds in glass cases. Wanda said the Historical Museum owned one of the world's largest collections. She explained that fairy crosses were found in only five places on earth, and Cherokee County was one of them. Southern Virginia was another, at Fairy Stone State Park near the Blue Ridge Parkway.

"Only five places?" I said. "Why?"

Wanda shrugged. "The legend of the Little People." She said the Little People and Moon-Eyed People may not have been one and the same, that there may have actually been two similar but separate beings. Or they could have been the same; the legend was tangled. But in any case, the Little People had cried and their tears had turned to stone, according to legend.

It was all very strange and bizarre, and I had lots to digest, at least two stories in one: the fairy crosses and the Moon-Eyed effigy, two figures formed from one stone. They still looked like aliens to me, and the whole thing sounded incredibly far-fetched. But the statue was here, right in front of my eyes, and pecked with a stone not carved with tools, because in ancient times there were no tools. Maybe one of the Moon-Eyed People had pecked their own image, theirs and that of their child. And I couldn't dismiss the fairy crosses, either, naturally formed and found only in five places—which was not just "according to legend." That part was true. Wanda showed me the documentation, and I even looked it up later. I found a surprising amount of information about the crosses online.

There was no denying what I was seeing, as preposterous as it all sounded. Wanda smiled and shrugged again. I don't think she was trying to convince me of anything per se but was merely laying out the odd discoveries that perhaps lent some believability to the legend.

I think she had also anticipated my questions and doubts. I was a reporter, after all, and reporters are skeptical. Plus, I was from big-city Raleigh, where people don't have time for such foolishness—Moon Pies maybe but not Moon-Eyed aliens. So, with a wise bit of forethought, she had invited a longtime professor of history to join us.

Billy Ray Palmer walked in just as I was finishing with Wanda. Billy Ray was his first name, a double name. He had taught for years at the local community college and was now retired, which is why he was able to meet us during the week—and, I supposed, why he came casual, dressed in an old tee shirt.

He leaned back in a chair, arrowheads and books behind him, and in a slow southern dialect repeated much of what Wanda had told me. But he did add some intriguing elements. "Now in 1803, Thomas Jefferson mentioned the Moon-Eyed People in his Indian Removal Act."

"Thomas Jefferson?" I said. I certainly hadn't expected Jefferson to be linked to Moon-Eyed People—or, rather sadly, to the Indian Removal Act. Here was the Trail of Tears again, the Removal Act a prelude to it. The Indians were to be forced from their land, and along with them, the little people with the strange moon eyes.

"I think the Moon-Eyed People, of course, were a real group of people," Billy Ray said, rocking back in his chair. "For whatever reason, they were muted somewhat." He was referring to their fair skin and round faces. "The effigy, I think, is a representation of them. I think they're twins, representing the Hiawassee and Valley Rivers." He said where the rivers joined, a village or mound had at one time existed, and that's where the Moon-Eyed People once lived—and where they had cried. "The legend says for each tear they shed, a fairy cross was formed."

I asked him what scientists said about the fairy crosses. He rocked in his chair. "It's a mystery to them also."

"Isn't it unusual that some of them form, perfectly form, a cross?"

"Perfect," he said.

I could see my news director rocking in his chair, too, shaking his head while he rocked. But the story or legend or mystery or whatever it was

had me. It was fascinating. And a bit sad. It was eerie looking at the aliens behind the glass, although, curiously, I found myself no longer thinking of them as aliens. A mother and daughter, perhaps—I could see that; it seemed to make sense. Or a father and son. Maybe the strange stone statue was all that remained of a race of people who had mysteriously vanished—or been cruelly banished.

"I guess it makes you think beyond yourself," I said to Wanda. "Maybe there were other people out there, beyond us."

She paused a long time before answering. "I think with God, all things are possible," she said at last and smiled.

"Do we just learn to keep an open mind?"

"Yes," she said. "Definitely."

MURPHY

THE MYSTERY OF ABRAHAM LINCOLN

I wasn't excited about history as a kid.

My social studies teacher was nearly as ancient as the people in my textbook. And he was all about the textbook—though I'm not sure he ever opened a spelling textbook. I don't think he realized the word *history* includes the word *story*.

It wasn't until ninth grade that I had a history teacher who taught with some fire in her belly. She spoke of Hitler overtaking one country after another and how, each time, the United States simply slapped his hand. That's how she put it. "Just slapped his hand," and she slapped her own hand—slapped it hard, too, and kept slapping it all the way to Pearl Harbor. Her poor hand was blazing red.

But I still felt uninspired with all those names and dates to memorize for exams. I'd shove them from my head as soon as I had checked the last multiple choice. The history seemed lifeless and the details dull. It wasn't until I became a reporter that I began to change—but not at first, not even then.

In the 1980s, I was working for the NBC affiliate in Winston-Salem, and I'd been sent to Central Prison in Raleigh to cover the execution of a death row inmate. It was a big story, and I was young, midtwenties, still green. I listened to the pre- and postexecution news conferences, covered the protest vigil, gathered file video of the crime scenes and victims, made sure I had all the important names and dates. I was ready for my eleven o'clock live shot. Fifteen minutes to go. And then the producer called me from the station. "Make sure you say what he had for his last meal."

"What?" I said. "His last meal?" But the producer was insistent.

I went on the air with my list of facts and figures, names and dates, t's crossed and i's dotted. "And for his last meal," I said, wincing as I did—the factoid seemed silly in comparison—"he ordered a dozen hot dogs all the way."

The next day at the station, the producer called me over, leaned on his desk, and looked me in the eyes. "Ten years from now," he said, "I won't remember anything about that case, not a thing—except for one thing. I'll always remember his last meal."

I remember, too, and it's been more than thirty years now. I remember because it gave an element of story to the history; it made it real.

I'll always remember a dozen hot dogs all the way.

I knew Abraham Lincoln was president during the Civil War and had freed the slaves. I even knew he'd been a Republican. But I actually thought John Wilkes Booth was more interesting, slipping into the theater, firing the fatal shot, leaping from the balcony, and galloping into the night.

When I worked for public television in Richmond, I traveled to Port Royal, Virginia, the place where Booth met his end, shot dead. The constables had killed the assassin and put the little town in the textbooks.

I must have read about Port Royal in school, but it was just another name. It was actually just another town, small and sleepy, when a photographer and I rolled in. I was in charge of a PBS newsmagazine back then, and on that particular day I was having a tough time finding anybody to interview. I finally corralled an auto mechanic, wired him up, and pitched

him questions as he stood beneath a car jacked on a lift and fiddled with a bad muffler. "What do you think, knowing Booth died here?"

The mechanic didn't say much. "Interesting. Yeah, it's history." The interview would have to do, though I wasn't quite sure if he was talking about Booth or the muffler.

But Port Royal, dead as it was the day I was there, actually came alive to me. We took video of a decrepit shed out in a field, wooden siding all busted up, the whole thing sagging to one side, and I could just see Booth holed up in there. It wasn't his actual hiding place, of course; he'd been burrowed in an old barn when the law found him and fired at him through the wooden planks. The shed we'd found would make for a suitable substitute on television, a way to help viewers visualize what had happened. It was just an old pitiful shack, but it stirred something in me. It stirred the story part of history.

It was actually a book that elevated my interest in Abraham Lincoln—not a textbook; I think I gave all those away. This was one called *Lincoln the Unknown*, though it wasn't the title that inspired me to read it but the author, Dale Carnegie.

He was the man who founded the famous course on poise and self-confidence. I took a Dale Carnegie class in Richmond and won the Lincoln book in a class contest on public speaking—granted, I had a leg up on my classmates since I routinely spoke to a television audience. Even so, the instructor made a show of presenting me the book and said it was reading material to inspire. I wanted to pass the class, so I read it.

If Dale Carnegie was a good speaker, he was also a good writer and researcher. I had no idea young Abraham had fallen head over heels for a pretty nineteen-year-old named Ann, and she with him. But their love was short-lived for Ann contracted typhoid and died. The loss practically killed Lincoln; in fact, he threatened to kill himself. For months after she died, he walked five long miles to her grave every day and would sit *all* day and mourn.

I thought about that as I stood by another grave outside a small chapel in Murphy, a grave inscribed with the name ABRAM. "Well, Abram, Abraham, Abe. You're gonna hear three different names," Wanda said—Wanda Stalcup, the woman from the Cherokee County Historical Museum who had told me about the Moon-Eyed People. I had returned to Murphy, and now she was telling me Abraham Lincoln's father might be lying under my feet. ABRAM ENLOE read the gravestone.

"The Enloes were lanky people," said Billy Ray—Billy Ray Palmer, the retired professor and historian from the Moon-Eyed People story had joined us also. "Six-foot-two, six-foot-three." He also told me that Abraham Enloe had been a farmer. "At their family farm in Rutherford County, they had a housekeeper, a teenager by the name of Nancy Hanks."

"Nancy Hanks became with child," Wanda said, and I noticed her eyebrows shoot up behind her glasses.

"With Abraham Enloe's child?" I asked.

"That's according to the legend," Billy Ray piped in. "You know, while Mrs. Enloe was away on several of her trips."

"The easiest thing to do . . . ," Wanda started to say, apparently fumbling for the right way to say it. "If they could just get rid of her . . ."

Abraham Enloe hatched a plan, Billy Ray said. "He got Tom Lincoln to take Nancy Hanks away with him." According to Billy Ray, Tom Lincoln had once lived in the area, and Tom and Nancy quickly left town together, moved to Kentucky, and married. "And young Abraham Lincoln was born."

It was a sunny spring day, the grass green, the tombstones shin high, some of them leaning, many with dates starting with 18. There were about fifty stones total scattered to the side of the chapel on a gentle slope by a quiet road. Abraham Enloe's gravestone was just a bit higher than most and had managed to remain straight despite its age; the first date etched on it started with 17. "Born 1770, Died 1840."

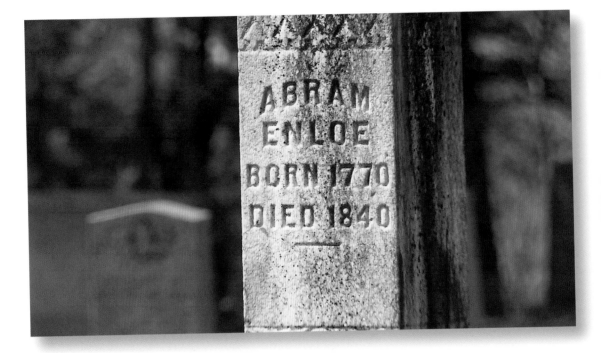

"Is it more than coincidence that Abraham Lincoln and Abraham Enloe are both named Abraham?" I asked Wanda.

Her eyebrows rose. "Suspicious to me. You know, that's just my opinion. There's a lot more names out there they could have chosen."

At the time, I thought I'd raised a solid bit of circumstantial evidence. Although I found out later that Tom Lincoln's father was also named Abraham.

"Have you seen pictures side-by-side of Abraham Enloe and Abraham Lincoln?" I asked Wanda.

She nodded. "I think there's a lot of resemblance myself."

Standing in that little graveyard, the lanky remains of Mr. Enloe resting beneath my sneakers, I had a pretty good hunch I was digging up a mound of controversy. For this was not my first Abraham Enloe story.

Enloe is actually a well-known name in Raleigh. There's Enloe High School, the name distantly linked to the Abraham buried in Murphy. Abraham Enloe visited Murphy often and on one of his trips became gravely ill. It was easier to bury him where he died—and perhaps the truth went with him to the grave.

I had seen photographs of Abraham Enloe and Abraham Lincoln side-by-side and thought it reasonable to presume the two men had belonged to the same family, that they could have even been father and son. They were both tall and had rather craggy faces. On the other hand, when Abraham Lincoln's photo was placed next to Tom Lincoln's, well, that was another striking comparison. Tom Lincoln was short and fat.

I had studied the comparisons when I visited the Lincoln Center in Rutherford County two years before my trip to the graveyard in Murphy. The Lincoln Center was a small white building in the tiny town of Bostic, largely dedicated to proving the sixteenth president was born not in Kentucky but in North Carolina.

"Was Abraham Lincoln born in a log cabin?" I asked the docent.

"Yeah," he said and pointed toward the window. "Probably the one up there on Puzzle Creek."

He told me the story of Nancy Hanks. "She birthed a son and named him Abraham." The docent believed the baby belonged to Abraham Enloe and his servant girl, Nancy. "An illegitimate child was not highly thought of," he said. "And so it's rumored Abraham Enloe provided Tom Lincoln with a wagon, a team of horses, and five hundred dollars." Off to Kentucky went Tom and Nancy. "And about their marriage . . . ," said the docent. "There was a boy with dark coarse hair at the wedding who, when they left the wedding ceremony, rode away with the newlywed couple in the wagon."

The Lincoln Center was loaded with documents, books, and photographs, including photos of John Wilkes Booth. "John Wilkes Booth kept a diary," the docent said. "There's an entry in that diary that he wanted to come to Rutherford County to explore Abraham Lincoln's roots."

I asked him if he thought there was a deliberate attempt to conceal the circumstances of Lincoln's birth, and he nodded rather vigorously. If born out of wedlock, he said, Lincoln might never have become president.

Now, by the little chapel in Murphy, Wanda and Billy Ray told me the same. "Back in those days, a lot of people might have held it against him," Wanda said. "But you know, it wasn't his fault. It wasn't his choice. It was a choice his mother made, and it's something he had to live with that reflected his entire life."

I thought again of the book Dale Carnegie wrote and of Lincoln's melancholy, which was said to pervade his entire life.

"And if he had never become president . . . ?" I asked Billy Ray.

"Oh, I don't even want to imagine."

I shifted and looked at my sneakers and felt a bit uneasy about standing over Abraham Enloe, for this now seemed like sacred ground, knowing the lanky man buried below may have impacted the whole course of American history. An exaggeration? Maybe it was. Conjecture? Sure.

Perhaps it was all just far-fetched fiction. Except I had seen the photographs. I had made the comparisons.

I knew there would be cynics scoffing at my Abraham Enloe story when it aired. They did the first time around as well with my story on the Lincoln Center. But it had been only a couple of cynics not many.

I asked Billy Ray about exhuming the bodies of Lincoln and Enloe and comparing their DNA. "What if you could?" I said. "Would you, or is it best to leave history alone?"

Billy Ray had spent years teaching history, and I gathered he was a knowledgeable, well-respected, local professor. He was also an easy-going, slow-talking, southern fellow. He took his time, looked around, and sniffed the air, and I couldn't blame him. I did, too; it was a gorgeous day. I thought Abraham Enloe would be pleased with his final resting place.

"You know the old mountain saying," Billy Ray said at last, and our eyes met, and then his fell upon the faded stone. Mine did, too. We both admired it. *Abram Enloe.*

"The old mountain saying . . . ," Billy Ray repeated softly. "Let sleepin' dogs lie."

THREE-POINT SHOT

THE FORGOTTEN MOMENT

Robert and I were checking out of our hotel on a late-winter morning in the North Carolina mountains, the end of another road trip. A successful one, too. We'd shot several stories to add to the stockpile and were ready to head back to Raleigh. We'd planned to shoot a couple more stories on the way. So once again, we were racing against the clock. We'd even forfeited our usual stop at Waffle House, a morning must, and opted instead for the quickie hotel grab-and-eat. I'm not a fan.

I've come to consider the hotel continental breakfast as one of the most wretched customs of American life. It's all elbows at the serve-yourself

counter. I duck and dodge, and somebody still bumps me, and it's a good thing I'm not holding a cardboard cup full of dark roast. I'm not because there's a line at the coffee machine, bunched up from folks taking their sweet time adding half-and-half and shaking their sugar packets for a full thirty seconds. When they finally tear the tops and tilt, they stand there and stir, around and around, oblivious to the caffeine-craved crowd behind them.

And the food? Watery scrambled eggs and limp undercooked bacon are the usual. I learned my lesson long ago and typically settle for a simple hard-boiled egg, thankfully already peeled, and an English muffin—except the dang toaster takes forever, and even the hard-boiled egg feels filmy, like it's been dipped in bath water.

So I was the first to scram from the breakfast nook that morning, exit the hotel, and make my way to the car, duffel bag in hand. Robert was dil-lydallying back in the lobby, which wasn't like him. He was always on time, in fact, usually ahead of time, while I was the one perpetually ten minutes late to everything—just ask my wife.

The automatic doors finally slid open, and out he walked with some-one by his side: a tall, thin man in a purple-and-gold jacket. I was waiting by the car for Robert to pop the lock with his remote, but he and the man were engaged in some sort of animated conversation—they were both smil-ing and nodding—and they even stopped under the overhang and talked a few minutes more. I was close enough to hear something about basket-ball, which didn't surprise me. The man was probably in his fifties and tall enough to have once played center. Also, March Madness was just around the corner. I figured they were wagering on which perennial favorite would make it the furthest: Duke or UNC.

"Western Carolina," Robert said, pointing a thumb behind him when he finally walked up. "He was at the game last night. Used to play for them, and now his son is playing."

"Oh," I said, opening the door at last, throwing in my bag, and climbing in the front. Robert was a Western Carolina grad, too, and I supposed the man's purple-and-gold colors had caught his eye, figured the two of them had rekindled a few memories from their college days. They might have even been in school at the same time.

"Yeah, and we were talking about the three-point game," Robert said, set-tling behind the wheel. "You know, I was at that game." He turned the key.

"What game?" I said, not totally interested in his answer; I was worried about being late to the next story. And the continental breakfast had left me feeling sour.

"The three-point game," he said as though I knew what he was talking about.

"Uh, huh." I checked my lunchbox for a granola bar.

"Yeah, I was there," he said. "First three-point shot in college history."

That last part hit me like a shot of the dark roast I never had. "What?"

"Oh, yeah. First time there'd been a three-point shot in college basketball. First time ever. First one." He backed out of the parking space.

"What do you mean?" I said. If it was common knowledge, I'd missed out.

He explained it to me as we rolled out of the lot and down the hill. He drove slowly because the hill was steep—the hotel, at least, had a beautiful view of the mountains. Robert was animated in describing the game even after his animated chat with the tall man. I was animated, too. I was about to jump out of the car. I told him to stop the car. I told him we should turn back. "I can't believe it," I said. "What a story."

"Yeah, it is," he said and shrugged. "But I never thought about it being a Tar Heel Traveler. I guess since I was there . . . It wasn't a big deal when it happened. And no one talks about it anymore. I don't know. But yeah, it's a great story."

I wanted to turn back and shoot it, shoot it now, but I knew we couldn't because we didn't have time. Robert knew it, too—he's always *on* time.

The light at the bottom of the hill was green, and we rolled on through while I considered our upcoming schedule. Maybe we could make another quick mountain trip, I thought, one before March Madness. What a sensational piece to air during the tournament. But March Madness was days away, too soon. Too much writing and editing to do in between.

By the time we hit the interstate, a sinking feeling had hit me in my hungry belly. The reality was, we'd have to wait another year, till next basketball season, before shooting the story. It would only make sense to air it then, right before the ACC tournament or March Madness again. I hated to wait, but I loved the story. Robert and I talked about it all the way to High Point, site of our next shoot.

We stopped for coffee along the way. No cream, no sugar. Black.

Maybe the extra time had been a good thing. It gave me a chance to track down some of the guys who had played in the historic game, who were actually on the floor during that key moment—the first official three-point goal in college basketball history. It happened November 29, 1980, in Reid Gym at Western Carolina. Until then, every basket made in college basketball counted as just two points no matter where on the court the player was when he launched the shot. The three-point shot was not part of the game.

And about that shot, *the* shot, the one for the history books—I even managed to find the player who sank it.

Robert and I spent almost a whole day driving to the mountains and stayed at the same hotel atop the hill. One year later, and I had my story. I was so excited I ordered cheese with my eggs the next morning at Waffle House.

We drove to Cullowhee and finally found a parking space on campus. Fortunately, Robert knew the way to Reid Gym; had we needed directions, I don't think most of the students could have helped us. Reid had apparently become a forgotten castoff, for there was now a state-of-the-art athletic complex, built in the years since Robert had graduated. It sat more than seven thousand people, hosted home games, and served as an entertainment venue. Bands such as Aerosmith, Bon Jovi, and Lady Antebellum had all performed at the Ramsey Center. The building was also an architectural icon with lots of glass and interesting angles.

Reid Gym, on the other hand, sat in a quiet corner of campus, a plain red-brick building. *Open only at the discretion of the building coordinator*, I had read online. So, I had called the school's public relations folks to let them know what we were up to—and to let us inside.

I never did meet the building coordinator, but the public relations staff had done a good job. They'd given me the name of a former staffer, the school's retired sports information director, a man who, as it turned out, had played a pivotal role in the historic three-point game.

That's who met us in the lobby. Except for the gray hair, Steve did not look at all like he was retired. He wore a sporty athletic shirt with "WCU" embroidered on the chest and a catamount growling between the letters. The catamount was the school mascot—I'd had to ask Robert what a catamount was. A cross between a lion and bobcat, he said, known to prowl the mountains of western North Carolina. I was suddenly glad I wasn't in the woods anymore searching for Eric Rudolph.

Steve pointed down the corridor, said the basketball court was at the end, and began leading the way. He didn't walk like he was retired, either. In fact, I found myself falling behind, though not entirely because of the quick pace. I kept peering inside the glass cases that lined the length of the hall. I saw big gold-plated trophies, team pictures, and signed basketballs—but not *the* basketball as far as I could tell. I was sure it would have been mounted on a pedestal with "First Ever Three-Pointer!" emblazoned on a brass plaque above it. I searched each case but saw no signs of anything related to the historic shot. I figured the school would have at least saved the net; players are always cutting down the nets, and surely, I thought, Western Carolina would have at least salvaged some frayed pieces of it. But I didn't see a single string.

I didn't see any old photos of the shot, no black-and-white freeze frames tracking the arc of the ball on its way to the hoop. Nor any that captured wide-eyed, open-mouthed fans. And, needless to say, no frozen *Swissshhh,* either.

I kept thinking maybe the next case, maybe the next, that there had to be an entire display devoted to the moment, but Steve had come to the end of the hall, and I'd soon run out of glass cases. We had stopped at a set of double doors, and Steve gave them a push.

The gym was big, shiny, and empty except for three men congregated near center court. The place was also filled with the potent smell of floor polish—the underworked building coordinator must have eagerly doused the hardwood with a few gallons.

The men were tall; two of them had me by a foot and the other by six or eight inches, and they were so absorbed in conversation, they didn't turn their heads when we walked in but rather kept right on talking and laughing. One of them even bounced on his toes and made shooting motions with his hands. He was the one wearing an old-timey black hat, which should have seemed extraordinarily out of place on a basketball court. Except it looked good on him, and so did the air ball in his hands—his motion was smooth; I'd even say elegant. If he'd had a real ball, no doubt about it—*Swissshhh!*

We were practically on top of them before they broke the circle and gripped Steve's hand and patted his arm. "Great to see you," they said at once, big smiles all around.

They leaned down and shook my hand, too, and Robert's, and the one with the black hat seemed especially glad to see us. "Ahhh . . . ," he said. "You guys . . ." His smile was nearly as wide as the gym, and he spoke in a coarse, whispery voice, which actually made him sound even more grateful than he already was—and he clearly was. He clapped a hand on my shoulder and thanked me for coming to tell the story. "It's a story that needs to be told," he said. "It's part of history. It needs to be known." He was spilling some powerful sound bites before we'd even turned on the camera.

He also kept using the word *documentary*. "Your documentary, Scott . . ." He said my name as if I was an old friend. "Scott, your documentary is going to get the story out." His smile grew even wider than before. "Ahhh," he said and squeezed my shoulder.

I smiled back but hunched under his grip, which had nothing to do with the squeeze. It's just that I couldn't bring myself to tell him that our "documentary" would last two-and-a-half minutes on the five-thirty news. And yet I agreed with him; I was sure the story was worth a documentary, for it was not only a compelling story but a forgotten one, which made it even more interesting. I began to silently strategize while standing there at center court.

Maybe the producer will give me three minutes. Maybe three and a half.

Ronnie Carr, Kevin Young, and Si Simmons had all been part of that historic moment, and now, more than thirty years later, they were back where it happened, in lonely Reid Gym reliving the lost past. I gathered they'd kept in touch over the years but that it had been awhile since they'd seen each other. And so that's why I backed away and started my interview with Steve under the basket, giving the trio a few minutes more to reunite. Thankfully, they kept the chatter low.

"This was a pilot program?" I asked.

"Well, it was experimental the first year," Steve said and explained that the Southern Conference had been the only one to try it out. And yes, it was strange, he said, a shot worth three points, but he had realized the potential. "This was a great way for a lot of publicity." He'd seen an opportunity; he saw it from the perspective of the sports information director he was then. Western Carolina had a good team in 1980, and any added press would be a bonus, national press especially. It could elevate the program even more.

That year, on the night of November 29, two other Southern Conference schools had a game; they were also part of the experiment. So it seemed inevitable that someone that night was bound to make history. The games were set to begin at 7:30 p.m.

Steve had struck me as efficient and well-organized. In the weeks before our trip, he'd helped me get in touch with the three players who now stood at center court. He'd kept the current public relations staff in the loop, made sure the building coordinator had left the door unlocked, and he had been on time, waiting for us in the lobby when we'd arrived. He must have exhibited equal skills thirty years before, not to mention extraordinary foresight.

It was his idea to move Western Carolina's game back one-half hour to 7 p.m. "This would give us a thirty-minute jump," he told me. "Move it to seven o'clock."

Western Carolina was hosting Middle Tennessee State that night. Middle Tennessee was a tough team, nationally ranked, and though it played in a different conference, it had agreed to allow the three-point shot for this particular game—the agreement was acceptable under college rules.

The game was huge. Reid Gym was packed. Robert had told me it was; he was in the crowd and remembered the excitement. Steve did, too. "And everybody was just sort of waiting for it to happen," Steve said, meaning the three-point shot.

"There were two shots taken earlier in the game," he said, "and both missed." Those two shots had been launched at least twenty-two feet from the hoop; the rules committee had adopted twenty-two feet as the experimental range for three points, and I could just imagine the collective, "Ohhhh!" of the crowd.

He told me what happened next, gave me the play-by-play, and described the shot—*the* shot. But the men who'd been part of the shot were standing a little more than three-point-range away from me, and I wanted them to tell it on camera. Plus, one of those men was the one who had made the shot. Steve understood but left me with a final thought—one, appropriately enough, about foresight. "Nobody had any idea that twenty-five, thirty years later the three-point field goal would be such a big thing." Western Carolina, he said, had started a revolution; the WCU Catamounts had changed college basketball forever.

"Coach wanted the opportunity for one of us to have that shot," Kevin Young told me—I had made my way to center court. Kevin was the shorter of the three but also the most talkative. "So Coach called time-out and designed a special play."

The game resumed. "I looked up, and Ronnie was wide open," he said.

"Wide open," added Si Simmons. Si was the tallest, lankiest of the three. "Wide open," he repeated.

"And I just threw the pass to him," said Kevin. He threw the pass to Ronnie Carr.

I looked at Ronnie, at Ronnie and his black hat, and this time there was no smile but rather intensity. I could see it in his eyes. And in his hands. "I just rose up, took the shot." He rose for the camera, rolled an invisible air ball off his fingertips, and followed its elegant arc to the basket, twenty-three slow-motion feet away. For a moment, nobody said anything.

"He got the shot off," Si finally said. "And it was nothing but net."

Ronnie's eyes were still locked on the basket. "And the rest," he said in a whisper, "is history."

It was Kevin who shattered the stillness of the moment, who broke the ice—ice not an altogether inappropriate word, even on a basketball court, for I suspected Ronnie had some ice in his veins, that when it was time to play he played, gave it his all, no distractions, eyes on the prize, trained on the hoop. *Swissshhh.*

"They stopped the game, recorded the time," Kevin said. He told me about the small ceremony at center court, right where we were standing, in fact. Somebody had taken pictures, but the time-out lasted just a minute or two because there was a lot of game left, and it was a vital game. One that Western Carolina won.

The underdogs had bumped off a nationally ranked opponent. It was a major deal and a big celebration; there'd be lots of headlines. It was only later in the locker room that talk turned to the three-point shot. Kevin remembered, "And we were like, 'Oh yeah, that was pretty cool what you did, man.'"

I watched him give Ronnie a friendly elbow, as he probably had that night long ago. Ronnie smiled at me, but the smile quickly vanished. "We didn't understand the relevance of that shot," he said and said it slowly in his sandpapery whisper, which somehow made what he said sound so much heavier and deeper. He brought his hands up again but not to take another invisible shot. "To keep that story alive it has to be brought to its . . ." He paused and held his hands near his face, held them like he was clutching a basketball, except there was no ball. "To its . . ." He was grasping for the right word. "Fullness," he finally said, hands cupping nothing but air.

The atmosphere had suddenly changed there at center court. I could feel it just as sure as I'd smelled the floor polish, and the feeling was potent. It was bitter. "You got Duke, you got Carolina. Well, you got Western Carolina," Kevin said and held up his index finger. "Oh yeah, my guy hit the first three-point shot in NCAA history."

"Do you feel that moment in history has been lost?" I asked, already knowing the answer. I'd known it in the hallway.

"Yeah, it's been lost," Si said. He was the quiet one, but I could distinctly hear his disappointment, his disgust.

But if there was a clear indication of just how miserably miniscule the moment had been treated, it was there on the floor, in the left corner of the gym, twenty-three feet from the basket. At the exact spot on the hardwood where Ronnie had hit the shot was a sticker. It was as round as a basketball, meant to mimic a basketball, but it was smaller, the colors predominantly purple and gold, the date of the game and the two opposing teams listed at the bottom of the outer rim. And at the top of the rim, it read, "College Basketball's First 3-Point Shot."

At the center of the sticker was Ronnie, Ronnie in black-and-white, Number 22 in midjump, the ball a half second from leaving his hands, a defender's hand reaching for the block but clearly too far away.

Here at last was a photo I'd been looking for, the actual moment, frozen and printed on the sticker stuck to the floor. I'd heard the moment had been captured with a movie camera, too—no doubt, Steve's foresight again. And why not go for maximum exposure by mailing the footage to the national Basketball Hall of Fame, where it could be shown for all to see? I had called the Hall of Fame, excited to have the footage for my story, but nobody there knew anything about it. The guy on the phone had never heard of Western Carolina and couldn't seem to grasp the historic significance of what I was talking about. But he said he'd do me a favor and check the archives. When I didn't hear back for two weeks, I called again. He said they didn't have it.

"But you've got to have it," I said. "It was the first three-point shot in college basketball history. It was huge."

"Dunno," he said.

It was lost. Nobody had it. When Western Carolina mailed the film, it had failed to make a backup copy. It couldn't have been Steve, I thought; no doubt somebody else from Western with no foresight at all.

So the still photo on the sticker was all there was, that small sticker on the floor of a basketball gym open only at the discretion of the building coordinator. I supposed it was a nice sticker as stickers went. But it was also pitiful.

"We made history," Si said. "It was always *we* made history." The team had indeed done so on that November night in 1980 at precisely 7:06 p.m. when Ronnie sank *the* shot. But thirty years later, almost nobody knew about it—including, it seemed, Western Carolina. Where was the banner hanging from the rafters? The commemorative display? The ceremonial photos snapped at center court immediately after the basket? All of that had apparently been lost, too, or had never existed.

We stood around the sticker, those three former players shaking their heads, and I felt for them. I wanted my story to set things right—in two and a half or three minutes. I wanted to call ESPN and say, "Hey, you guys should do a documentary on this." Ronnie would have been proud of me, a documentary at last. But who was I to ESPN? Just some no-name news reporter. I could already hear the response, "Dunno."

But the documentary that might never be told wasn't the saddest part. The players shaking their heads wasn't the saddest—although that was awfully sad. The sticker wasn't the saddest part, either.

We stood looking at the floor a long time. Robert rolled on the sticker from several angles—we knew we wouldn't have much video to tell our story. I studied the old photo in the center, Ronnie taking the jumper, and I realized, rather ironically, that that was the saddest part of all. Not the shot, of course—*the* shot.

No, the saddest part was what happened to Ronnie Carr.

THREE-POINT SHOT

WHAT HAPPENED TO RONNIE

"I was known as a shooter," he said.

I had taken Ronnie aside, and we sat on a bleacher. I don't think Kevin and Si minded; they knew Ronnie's story. I had learned about it myself in my research and was surprised. It was related to the three-point shot but, really, was another story entirely, and I was already thinking two stories in two parts: the three-point shot and Ronnie Carr on consecutive nights—if the producer didn't have a conniption.

"Were you considered one of the best basketball players in the country at that time?" It was another question I already knew the answer to; I'd read up on him.

"Yes, I was."

He talked about the good teams Western Carolina had back then. "They were known. They were still considered mid-major."

In 1980, when Ronnie hit the three-point shot, he was a six-foot-three-inch sophomore who would go on to be the conference scoring leader that season, averaging more than seventeen points per game. The next year, he averaged nineteen and led the conference again. Heading into his senior year, Ronnie was listed as the league's preseason player of the year.

Ronnie told me the pros had long been looking hard at him, and he figured the NBA was his future, maybe a first-round pick. He certainly had the numbers, having scored almost fifteen hundred points in three seasons. "I put everything I could into basketball."

In the summer before his senior year, he received an invitation to attend Dean Smith's basketball camp in Chapel Hill. While at camp, he received a second invite: a cookout dinner with Michael Jordan and other famous athletes.

Ronnie climbed in his car and turned onto Highway 15-501. It was a rainy night, and he wasn't sure of the directions. He thought he might be lost. And then he almost was.

"All I remember was seeing just a big flash of light coming to my driver's side," he said in that sandpapery whisper. "The impact was so devastating it tore my left mitral valve." It tore the valve from his heart, requiring immediate open-heart surgery. Plus, he'd broken both arms, both legs, both collar bones, and severely fractured his wrist and ankle.

A police cruiser had smashed into his car.

"Was he chasing somebody?" I asked.

Ronnie shook his head. "Well, that was his alleged story, but he didn't have any sirens on, and he was out of his jurisdiction." Apparently, there was quite a bit of controversy and lawsuits. The officer walked away that night uninjured.

"How close to death were you?"

Ronnie looked me in the eyes. "Very close," he said—he whispered. "Very close." He'd been twenty-one years old, and his basketball career was finished.

"We're really talking about two moments that impacted your life: the three-point shot and the wreck?" I said.

"It changed my life. It changed my life for the better."

I thought I'd heard wrong at first or that he'd misspoken. "For the better?"

He kept his eyes on mine. "It's allowed me opportunities to work with kids and tell people my story." To tell them, he said, about the famous three-pointer, the historic shot he took—*the* shot. And the catastrophic shot he took—the crash. "And I've learned to give back based on what has happened to me, to overcome and be successful."

He talked quite a bit about the foundation he had started, the Ronnie Carr Foundation, to help inspire and motivate youth up and down the East Coast. His voice rose above a whisper when he talked about it. He'd become a motivational speaker and had devoted his life to helping children realize their potential, conquer adversity, and achieve their dreams. He had put basketball behind him, had been forced to, but he had found a greater calling. He told me he was sure he was making a difference.

Despite the wreck, the trauma, the multiple surgeries, the Atlanta Hawks drafted Ronnie in 1983 with the tenth pick in the tenth round, even though his injuries were so severe he had to sit out his senior season in college. However, when he'd torn his heart valve, doctors had to replace it with an artificial one, and the risk of competing in the NBA was too great. He was drafted but never played. Although his career comes with a positive asterisk, too. He played just three seasons at Western Carolina, and yet to this day Ronnie Carr remains ranked as one of the school's all-time leading scorers.

"Do you think that first three-point shot was really a little more than just about basketball?" I asked, though not altogether sure what exactly

I was asking but just fishing for some deeper meaning. Of course, I knew what the three-point shot had become, how important it was to the game of basketball. It had changed the game, was embedded in the game, routine. Nobody thought anything of it anymore. But it had started with Ronnie.

"Ahhh," he said at my question and smiled. "Ahhh, Scott, that overwhelms me when you say that, because it was." I could see it was in his face: the meaning, the pride, and whatever else was there. Ronnie was in the history books, even if he wasn't on ESPN or hanging from the rafters at Western Carolina. He had done something special, and it had led to something special: his work with children. Ronnie's life-changing moment at 7:06 p.m., November 29, 1980, had, perhaps, helped changed so many other lives. And yet, Ronnie said, it was just a normal shot, nothing out of the ordinary.

That's what he said, but his face told a different story—a happy, grateful, successful story despite what happened later. "Ahhh," he said again, and that smile of his grew as wide as the gym floor. "Other people attempted that shot, but they didn't make that shot," he whispered. It was Ronnie Carr who had made it.

Yes, Ronnie Carr had made it.

BASKETBALL PHENOM

BINGO!

Another basketball story. A five-year-old phenom.

He was forty-eight inches tall, hitting a ten-foot-high hoop, and the kid couldn't miss. Every time he took a shot—bingo!

Josiah was a cute kid, scrambling around the gym in his baggy uniform, slipping between defenders twice his size and twice his age. His dad had gathered a group to play pickup, and some of the kids weren't bad. But it was obvious Josiah was the dynamo—quick, slithery, and accurate—and a proud preschool graduate. He'd soon be headed to kindergarten. Bingo!

It was summertime in Wilmington, and what fun it was watching Josiah play while his dad cheered him on. "It's more than just putting the ball in the hoop," his dad told me. "We're trying to groom him into being the correct man, of good character. You know, we're teaching the 'Yes, ma'am, no, ma'am.'"

His dad had once been a talented player himself, and now he was coaching Josiah—and maybe thinking the NBA might be in his little boy's future. "Easily top five all-time," he said, meaning he was sure his four-foot son was among the best five-year-old basketball players ever.

We could have spent all day shooting Josiah. He was dazzling. The other kids towered over him, but I think they were impressed, too. His teammates kept passing him the ball, and why not? Bingo! Meanwhile, the kids on the other team, rather than putting their arms in the air to block his shots, began to put their hands on their hips and simply watch. They also watched the score turn lopsided. It was time for them to call time-out, which gave me time to sit Josiah down for an interview.

I don't know what I was thinking. I guess I was thinking a kid with that many moves on the court would be equally outstanding on camera. I think I forgot he was five years old.

I spent the next twenty minutes asking Josiah every question I could think of—it was a long time-out—and during that time he opened his

mouth only once. He uttered just two words; after twenty long minutes, just two measly little words. "It's fun." The basketball phenom was phenomenally bashful.

All of a sudden, my story seemed as sunk as the ball from one of Josiah's jump shots. Nobody wins a basketball game by scoring only two points, and I had no idea how to pull off a story on a player who spoke only two words, not even if his talent did the talking for him.

I did have his dad's interview, so there was that. "We have the privilege of waking up to him every day," Josiah's dad said, "spending time with him every day, like every day is a vacation for myself and his mother." It was good sound, but, still, I had almost nothing from Josiah—lots of nothin' but net but little else. I said my goodbyes feeling smaller than he was and as dejected as the other team.

I never want to shoot a story and not use it. No throwaways for me; that would be like tossing up an air ball. So when I returned to the station, I wrangled over how to save the story and began by studying the video.

There was Josiah again: dribbling, shooting, scoring. But I noticed something I hadn't paid attention to when we were there: his facial expressions. He had a great smile; his smile lit up his whole face, and I began logging all his smiles, noting where they were on the video. Then there were his

head shakes and nods. Robert had also captured him during a break, sitting on the ball, yawning—a big yawn—and burying his face in his hands. Once again, I'd forgotten he was only five. Nap time!

I wrote to the video. I wrote to the shots he made. *"Bingo,"* I announced in the audio booth. *"It's been a long day,"* I said when he yawned. *"But Josiah has a long, happy life ahead of him."* Over that line, Robert edited a camera shot taken from the basket's perspective. There was little Josiah, launching the ball from twenty feet away. And once again, nothin' but net!

I'd been forced to pull a rabbit out of a hat. Josiah was a magician with the ball, but the story's secret was in its disguise. Writing to the video provided a mask; it helped hide the fact that all he ever said was "It's fun." My words fit his facial expressions—they edited together beautifully—and those expressions of his were adorable. Josiah and I made a heck of a team.

The story's closing shot featured him, all forty-eight inches of him, facing the camera, cradling the basketball between his arm and hip, and smiling his biggest smile yet. That was the best shot of all, the money shot.

Bingo!

STATESVILLE STAINED GLASS

CHRISTOPHER

I went to do one story and found another.

Someone emailed me about a story idea in Statesville, which came at a good time since Robert and I were planning a trip in that direction. It had been a while since we'd visited Statesville, and I felt badly about ignoring such a decent-sized town, home to twenty-five thousand people, forty miles north of Charlotte.

The story was about a stained glass company, and I immediately envisioned people cutting and painting. I'd seen the process before, all done by hand, and knew it was both meticulous and colorful work.

I called Statesville Stained Glass and talked with owner Dennis Lackey. "You're welcome to come anytime," he said and assured me there'd be lots going on for us to shoot.

We picked a date and time and were all set, and normally I would have hung up and moved on to other things, but Dennis seemed grateful for my call, and so we chatted a bit longer. He told me how honored he was to be part of such meaningful glass work; the company primarily did windows

for churches. I asked how long he'd been in the business, even though I knew I'd pose that same question when I sat down to interview him. He explained that it was his son who had led him to the company. He said his son was six years old and had passed away.

I didn't get the full story over the phone. It actually threw me a bit. I was going for a simple feature about the art of making stained glass—and maybe it was best to keep it simple; I wasn't sure.

Before we said our goodbyes, Dennis gave me his company's address. It was on Christopher Lane.

Dennis was a stocky man with glasses, gray hair, and a mustache. His wife worked in the office, too, their desks practically side by side, just the two of them in a room apart from the factory, though "factory" makes it sound like a routine assembly line, which was not the case.

He led us through a door into a warehouse, and yet "warehouse" sounds like some cavernous hole. That wasn't the case, either, although the place did have a gritty feel. I saw men and women stretched over long tables, measuring and drawing, their fingertips smudged black. Jesus lay on one table, inked on white paper.

Dennis pointed out the painted glass, some panes as big as he was, and I marveled at scene after scene of glorious colors and angels. I think he saw how impressed I was and hefted a piece up to a window so I could witness the light streaming through. The effect was dazzling, the colors made even more vibrant and profound.

"Make yourself at home," he said before walking back through the door. I appreciated his trust but felt uneasy surrounded by all that precious glass,

especially when I saw Robert leaning over an artist's shoulder. I hoped he had a tight grip on the camera.

There were half a dozen artists, both men and women; "artists" is the term Dennis had used, and yet they tended to speak in technical terms, which seemed to contrast with the loftiness of their subject matter. But then again, they had a job to do and seemed serious about it. They labored among angels every day and strained to make them look as real as possible, or as real as they imagined.

Robert roamed about, lingering on the glass cutter. I watched the man prepare to snap a curvy piece off a large pane and winced when he made the cut, but it was clean, not a single stray shard.

The artists were actually apologetic. They weren't doing any painting that day, which they said would have been great for us to capture. And it would have been; in fact, painting the glass should have been central to the whole feature, but reporters are sometimes forced to make do with what they have and camouflage what they don't. I felt that all the other action, plus the finished windows, might be sufficient—those beautiful windows would carry the story.

All I needed now was to interview Dennis. He could provide me the background on the company and tell me where all that magnificent glass ended up.

"Churches and universities across the United States," he said.

We sat in his office, his chair conveniently positioned in front of a sample of stained glass resting on the windowsill behind him. He said the company had created windows for Duke Chapel and other prominent buildings, and he gave credit to his staff and their remarkable talent.

Dennis was a nice man though somewhat somber and reflective. Or maybe I was just thinking about the death of his son. Was that it, his son's death hovering over the conversation?

After more than three decades of interviewing people, I have learned to read them, and I found myself reading Dennis's body language. He rubbed his temple with two fingers, and I could see him thinking, his mind working. He spoke slowly, often pausing several seconds between sentences, gaps aching with silence.

Even the room itself seemed still, though I was conscious of Dennis's wife just a few feet away, sitting at her desk and no doubt eavesdropping on the interview. The stillness seemed especially heavy and not just because of the two big desks dominating much of the office. There was something else in the room. *Emptiness?* Or not in the room. *His son?*

Trust is a delicate thing between reporter and interviewee, sometimes hard to win and easy to lose. I didn't ask Dennis about his son. Instead, I asked about himself and, again, about how he came to own the company in the first place.

"We never took it serious," he said about the previous owner approaching him about buying it. "I had been in a totally different industry. I can't draw a straight line, but these people can." He pointed to the wall, meaning the artists on the other side, and was suddenly more animated. For the first time I felt I might be nearing *his* other side, whatever might be behind *his* wall. "My intent was not to be here past fifty-five or sixty years old, and that's come and gone, but I love it. This is our ministry here."

I heard *ministry* and sat a bit straighter, for the word felt like my window. "Tell me about your son."

Dennis drew in a deep breath, and normally a pause such as that would have made me question my own question—although I hadn't asked a question. "Tell me about your son." Period. The statement felt right, and so did the timing. It was more of an offering, allowing Dennis a window of his own.

"We lost Christopher when he was six years old. The doctor called us in and said, 'I really hate to tell you this, but he's got three to four months.'" Dennis explained that Christopher had leukemia and died in 1980—more than thirty years ago. "It's just like it was yesterday."

"Do you ever ask why?"

He must have asked himself that same question every day since, and yet he drew another long breath before answering. "We're not supposed to do that, but in the back of your mind you have to. And you just . . . You just have to move on."

And so Dennis and his wife, Sylvia, bought the stained glass company.

"We had to do something to change our lives, and that's why we're here. We believe God put us here." He believed God had opened a window. "We love it. We absolutely love it."

I asked if he had a picture of his son, and Sylvia brought me one—she *had* been listening and gave me a pleasant smile. "It's grainy," she said, admiring the snapshot she'd no doubt viewed a thousand times. "But I think he looks so handsome."

The picture showed Christopher leaning against a tree, dressed in what looked like church clothes. He wore a white bow tie and a shy grin, though I had to study it closely. The photo *was* grainy, but I was grateful we at least had one. We'd need it for the story.

It was a different story now, no longer just about a stained glass company. It was more about Dennis and how he'd been led toward the light. It wasn't easy asking about his son, probing that painful layer, but I'd learned over the years that those who've experienced  loss often appreciate the interest, for too many people, including their own friends and family, often *don't* ask.

Stories with layers are the best kind, and even as Dennis continued talking, I was scripting it in my head: Open with video of artists designing the colored panes before revealing their finished work. Only then would I reveal the death of Dennis's son. Christopher's passing would add unexpected poignancy and depth, and Dennis's own story would give it meaning. But Dennis wasn't done.

"With the churches' permission, we always use his face on one of the children." He was telling me that Christopher was often painted onto the stained glass, his image depicted in various scenes on the windows. The face of one of the children was Christopher's face. "It's all over the country." Worshippers nationwide bore witness to the little boy who by then had been gone thirty-five years.

Dennis showed me one of the windows, a beautifully painted garden scene with Jesus at its center. Jesus was seated, clad in white with a billowy red robe draped across his knees, and he was holding the hand of a small boy. The boy wore blue shorts, a white shirt, and warm smile, which Jesus gently returned. It was a touching scene, comforting and peaceful. Jesus was blessing him; his other hand rested on the boy's head, a boy with blond hair as bright as the sun. This was but one example, Dennis said, his eyes never leaving the window. He smiled, and I understood why. Every time he saw his son, he saw him in heaven.

A day or two later, Dennis emailed me, thanking me for our visit but concerned. He had assumed we'd captured the artists painting the glass. Not until he had a chance to speak to them did he realize we'd missed the painting process altogether. He apologized for the miscommunication and urged us to return, said he would accommodate us at any time and was certain our viewers would appreciate the artistry it took to hand paint each pane.

Dennis was right, of course. We'd missed the most critical part, though I'd been confident about overcoming the omission with all the other video we'd gathered.

Statesville was a long way from Raleigh, more than two hours west, and I had no idea when we'd be traveling that way again, but I told Dennis we'd try to return soon. Sometimes the story is worth the wait.

I held on to Christopher's story for three months—it had become *his* story. There had been deadlines and editing to do, and it took us that long to finally break free. It was a quick visit this time, and the artists were indeed painting; they were painting Jesus. But our return came with another surprise: Christopher.

Dennis and Sylvia were ready with a much better photo. Christopher's face filled the frame: blond hair, blue eyes, happy smile—such cute little-boy teeth—the picture absolutely radiant with joy and innocence. I knew then my story was complete.

And, yes, it was about the story, because Christopher would be viewed on screen as he was on glass, forever young and alive and with Jesus. And because of our story, thousands of people would come to know his.

"Do you feel Christopher's presence?"

Dennis paused before answering, but this time the pause was brief. "We know we'll see him again," he said and nodded. He continued nodding, slowly, assuredly—a silent moment more powerful than words.

FAMOUS LOUISE'S ROCK HOUSE RESTAURANT

THREE COUNTIES UNDER ONE ROOF

Sometimes the layers of a story are all under one roof.

I had heard about a restaurant in the mountains, a famous restaurant: Famous Louise's Rock House Restaurant. Its location made it famous. Famous Louise's straddled three counties, and all three intersected inside that little building. The building itself was remarkable, for much of the Rock House was made of rocks.

We parked across the street between two signs, reflective green ones with shimmery letters, especially shimmery since it was a sunny summer day. The sign twenty yards to my right announced WELCOME TO AVERY COUNTY, LEAVING BURKE COUNTY. The one twenty yards to my left read LEAVING BURKE COUNTY, WELCOME TO MCDOWELL COUNTY. There was even a third

sign, which read LINVILLE FALLS, which I was glad to see; it was comforting to know exactly where we were—our location was becoming confusing.

In front of me was the restaurant, not just a little roadside diner, but more like a country-style house with large, flat, sandy-colored stones cemented across the bottom half of the building. The upper half was shingled, and so was the roof, which draped over the eaves. The place looked inviting, even though it sat by itself with no other buildings around—though there sure were plenty of signs around. I walked across the blacktop, past the 183/221 markers. I had also arrived at the meeting point of two state roads.

The screen door squeaked when I opened it, and I made a mental note to mic the door later—a good screen-door squeak can do wonders for a restaurant story. I walked in and looked around and spotted three signs dangling from different areas of the ceiling. An Avery County sign hung from one corner, Burke from another, McDowell from a third, completing the overhead triangle. Although each sign was shaped like a rectangle, painted pale green with white letters neatly stenciled onto the wood. The signs looked homey, and so did the restaurant.

There was lots of wood, ruffled curtains, and whirring ceiling fans. Yellow and orange daisies poked from Mason jars at each table, and most of the tables were occupied. It was lunchtime in the mountains, and I noticed T-shirts and shorts—and meatloaf and mashed potatoes. I made another mental note: to eat before I left.

I had entered under the Burke County sign but crossed into McDowell County to ask for the owner who soon appeared from Avery County.

"Louise?" I asked.

"No," she said. "I'm Shirley. Louise is my mom. She's retired but came in special just for you." She turned to the table beside us where a woman with a full head of white hair looked up with a pleasant squint and extended her hand. "Please," she said and invited me to sit. Shirley, meanwhile, said she'd be back in a bit and hurried away.

Louise wore a checkered sweater, multicolored, and I couldn't decide whether it was perfectly appropriate or perfectly odd. It was still summer and hot for a sweater but fitting because the checkered squares intersected. She looked good in purple, green, and white while seated at the junction of Burke, McDowell, and Avery.

"I've always loved this place," Louise said and looked around at what she had built, tucking her arms in and scrunching her shoulders like people do when they're cold. Except I sensed the opposite was true. I think Famous Louise's warmed Louise. "I've really loved this place ever since I've been here."

Louise was such a nice and friendly lady, but I talked with her for just a few minutes because people were still coming in, and waitresses kept whisking by our table with loaded trays. Robert and I needed to record some of that action on camera, and so I thanked Louise—"I love this place," she said again—and I exited McDowell and made my way into Avery.

The food looked fantastic: mountain trout, chicken salad, country ham, green beans. "Our burgers are great," said one of the waitresses, a college-age brunette. All the waitresses were young and cute, and I gathered it was a fun summer job before school started again.

"You must be tired," I teased. "You know, walking through three counties."

She giggled and nodded. "To get them their food and serve them their food."

I had to admit, the pot roast looked mighty tempting, as did the Calabash Shrimp and Pimento Cheese Sandwich.

I at last crossed into Burke and corralled Shirley, who appeared constantly on the go except when chatting with customers. She bopped from table to table, county to county, and seemed to know just about everybody.

"Here's a little history of the restaurant," she said and pointed to a wall decked with black-and-white photos. "It all began with this tree."

The tree was a skinny, spindly thing without any branches. I was surprised someone back then had even bothered to take a picture of it. "The three counties met there, and moonshiners drank there," she said and smiled. "Well, they got tired of getting rained on, so in 1936 they built a building, and when the revenuers would come from whichever county, they would just move over to the other side of the building." She smiled wider, and when she raised her palms, I could tell she meant *Home free!* "They'd just walk over to the other county. Good to go!"

I asked her more about the unusual convergence of all three counties. "You walk in the door through Burke County," she said. "Most of the kitchen is in Avery County. If you go to the restroom, that's in McDowell County. But now when you flush, it goes through Burke and over into the landfill in Avery." She raised her palms again and flashed a big smile.

I asked about the food, all that good country cooking—breakfast, lunch, and dinner. And the pies; I'd seen some of the waitresses cut whopping slices of cherry and apple. "Oh, my gosh," Shirley gushed, and this time clapped her palms to her chest. The pie was homemade, too, she said, and so were the jams and jellies. She pointed to rows of colorful jars propped on the windowsills around the restaurant. I went to take a closer look and read "Homemade Peach" and "Strawberry Rhubarb" and debated which to bring home to my wife.

I accidentally bumped the arm of a man at a table whose hamburger steak caught my eye first. But then I looked up and saw his long curlicue mustache. "What county are you sitting in, do you know?" I asked.

He checked the overhead sign. "Burke."

"Well, your mustache might be in two counties."

He laughed. "You're absolutely right from where I'm sitting."

I noticed somebody wearing a T-shirt that read "Here's to the Good Times" and told Robert to get a shot of it, then pulled out my notepad and wrote what I thought might be my story's closing line: *"Here's to the good times at Famous Louise's Rock House Restaurant."*

Good times and good food. I ended my visit with a full belly—the Reuben sandwich had hit the spot.

I pulled open the squeaky screen door and stepped outside and before I left made sure to study the rocks cemented into the building. Shirley had told me to hunt for different shapes. I poked around and at last found the round rock, a perfect circle. Then I spotted the romantic rock, shaped like a heart. But I was most excited by my third find, the rock with three pointed ends—it was shaped like a triangle.

Three points within one.

THE HEN & THE HOG, AND THE HALIFAX RESOLVES

PATRIOTISM AND SHRIMP AND GRITS

"How many people live in Halifax?" I asked.

"Two hundred thirty-four," she said, shaking her head with each syllable as if to say, *That's it. Teeny tiny.* And yet her smile revealed pride and gratitude—at least, it did to me. I could practically read her thoughts: *Just 234, but I sure am lucky to live here.*

I was aware of the town's role in the American Revolution and knew April 12 was as dear to Halifax as the Fourth of July. In fact, every April, around the first of the month, somebody from up that way would zip me an email that said, "You covering the anniversary this year?" Then around the middle of the month, they'd fire off another note: "Didn't see your camera. So disappointed."

Revolutionary history doesn't usually translate well to television. I worry that if all viewers see are paintings of men in wigs, they'll punch the remote.

But I changed my mind in April 2018, and I must admit, the reason I did was not exactly due to the great historical significance of the date but because of the delicious promise of a glorious lunch.

I began receiving other emails that said, "You need to visit a restaurant in Halifax called The Hen & The Hog," and I immediately pictured farmers in overalls at splintery tables and chefs in bloody aprons clutching meat cleavers. But the emails kept coming, and I learned the place was actually quite upscale. Somebody gushed over the shrimp and grits. Someone else raved about the beef fillet.

In the end, it wasn't the history that lured me to Halifax; it was my stomach.

The restaurant was big and spacious, a wide-open, two-story room with a high ceiling painted white and several white ceiling fans gently whirring. The whiteness lent a clean, sophisticated look, although the place also had a days-of-old, tavern-like feel, especially because of its wooden floor, the wood dark and boards creaky.

The floor stretched all the way to a staircase at the opposite end of the room, a staircase with no walls, just rails. The steps themselves were also wood, bluish-gray, and unusually wide.

The staircase was a focal point but not the only one, for the steps traveled up to a huge American flag painted on the second-floor wall. On either side of it were two other murals, also American flags, though slightly smaller and somewhat different than the one in the middle. The stars and stripes were there but not as many, and on one flag the stars formed a circle in the upper left-hand square.

At first I thought it was a man who owned The Hen & The Hog. Glenn was the first name; a farmer, I figured—Farmer Glenn come to Halifax to fry up some hens and hogs. But Glenn was a female who greeted me at the door with a smile, a woman in her midfifties with brown hair, wearing a black turtleneck with a beaded necklace. She looked rather fashionable and spoke with a pleasant, lilting voice that was both southern and congenial.

She started to show me around but stopped to introduce me to some people at some of the tables. I could see right away it was a distinguished crowd. I met men in collared shirts and V-neck sweaters and women with knitted scarves and pretty blouses.

The food appeared upscale, too. The shrimp and grits did indeed look inviting. And so did the burger, one far more glorified than McDonald's.

I heard Glenn's friends call her by a different name. They called her Patterson. "Glenn Patterson Wilson," she explained when I asked. She said she'd gone by Glenn in her previous career, but in Halifax it was Patterson to avoid confusion—her mom was Glenn. In fact, she introduced me to her mom, who happened to be at one of the tables, though I wondered if her mother had come for the tomato pie or to eavesdrop on her daughter's interview.

I suggested a countertop table for the interview, and Patterson and I sat on stools, and Robert framed her with the stairs over her shoulder. I saw that each step bore the name of a state spelled prominently across each riser: North Carolina, Virginia, Pennsylvania . . . "The thirteen colonies?" I asked, and she nodded—I'd made sure to count the stairs before I asked.

"To think that the first formal call for independence from Great Britain happened right here in Halifax," she said and once again shook her head, and I agreed it was hard to believe. The independence of America had started in this little town.

Halifax had been a major port town in 1776 because of its proximity to the Roanoke River. That was at a time when colonists were restless to sever ties with the king, although no colony had formally declared its intention to seek freedom; none had actually put it in writing—not until North Carolina initiated that first bold step.

Three months before the Fourth of July, political leaders from the state journeyed to Halifax, eighty-three men with names such as Jones, Nash, Burke, and Harnett. No one is quite sure where they gathered, but some have theorized it was at a local tavern. After all, they were putting their lives at risk, committing an act of treason against the king, and they might have needed a few good belts of whiskey.

They hammered out a statement—"*A government springing wholly from the people*," read one notable line—and on April 12, 1776, the group voted unanimously to adopt it. They called their declaration the Halifax Resolves.

"It was the first spark that gave the founding fathers the confidence to sign the Declaration of Independence three months later," Patterson said and bopped her fist on the tabletop. "That's pretty darn special."

In fact, some historians believe Thomas Jefferson wrote parts of the Declaration of Independence based on the Halifax Resolves, that he used the Resolves as a model when crafting the Declaration. The two documents sound alike—their tone and language are similar—but, of course, the Resolves came first.

Jones, Nash, Burke, Harnett and Washington, Jefferson, Franklin, Adams. Halifax natives insist the former were just as smart and courageous as the latter. The latter are rightly revered, the names of the founding fathers proudly engraved on monuments. And if it's any consolation, the names of some of the Resolves men are printed on state maps. Jones, Nash, Burke, and Harnett are names of North Carolina counties.

Waitresses whisked by our table, and I heard lots of lively chatter and turned to take in the party-like atmosphere, the whole place seemingly full of good friends. I looked at all those happy people and wondered where everybody had come from. I also wondered about the pimento cheese fritters with red-pepper-jelly sauce.

I was impressed by how The Hen & The Hog had managed to balance a saucy modern vibe with a rustic historic feel. But then, Glenn Patterson Wilson had struck her own curious balance—and not just with her first and second names.

She'd grown up in Halifax, and April 12 had always been a fun part of her childhood. The day was a big deal, a celebration that each year drew festival-goers from across the state. People would dress up in colonial costumes and cheer passionate speakers who delivered patriotic speeches. There was plenty of good food and music, and WRAL celebrities often attended, including such beloved personalities as news anchor Charlie Gaddy and longtime farm reporter Ray Wilkinson. In fact, Ray was so taken with the history that he became head of the Halifax Restoration Association, even though he didn't live in Halifax.

But while Patterson cherished the colonial festivities, she was also drawn to England, especially after a high school trip to Europe. She told her mom she wanted to study overseas and enrolled at Richmond College near London, where she majored in fine arts and later earned a degree in interior design.

After graduation she settled in the Washington, DC, area and landed a job with Marriott International. It was good timing, for Marriott was in the midst of a huge growth spurt. Patterson was just twenty-three years old and soon found herself designing hotels, everything from lobbies to restaurants to guest rooms. It was a career that would take her around the globe.

"One time, I was giving the prime minister of Fiji tours of our project, and I would be thinking, *What has happened? I'm from Halifax!*" she said and laughed.

She worked closely with Bill Marriott Jr., the company's executive chairman. Bill had started his career working at his family's little restaurant chain and over time transformed it into one of the world's largest lodging companies.

Patterson's work kept her busy, though she would occasionally return home to see her mother, and when she did, she couldn't help but notice the town's steady decline. First one store closed and then another until eventually all that was left in downtown Halifax was the bank, post office, and a small antiques store. And then the antiques store went up for sale.

It seemed that even the annual Halifax Day celebration had begun to peter out. The April anniversary didn't draw the crowds it used to, and Patterson feared people had forgotten the town's important Revolutionary past.

And yet, the April 12 date is boldly scrolled on the state flag. There it is, below the N and the C, "April 12th, 1776" highlighted inside a wavy yellow ribbon. But Patterson began to wonder if anybody even noticed the date on the flag, or if they did, whether they had any idea what it meant.

She thought about those vacant, rotting buildings in downtown Halifax and told herself somebody ought to do something. Perhaps she reflected on those early colonists who had helped change the world. Maybe she thought of Bill Marriott, who'd built an empire nearly from scratch. Whatever it was, something stirred inside her, and she realized if somebody was going to do something, that somebody would have to be her.

"Did people think you were crazy?" I asked.

"They did. They thought I had lost my mind."

She bought one of those buildings in 2014, one with gaping holes in the roof that let rain pour in. "You could see the sky. It was a huge undertaking."

She undertook it. She continued working for Marriott but would spend nights drawing up plans. She hired contractors and on weekends would drive down from her home in Maryland to oversee the work.

At first she didn't know exactly what she was designing. She knew the town needed a gathering space and finally settled on a restaurant. Then she needed a name, something that suggested North Carolina. She thought of the state's long tradition of barbecue and agriculture, but she also remembered the cozy feel of English pubs, places with names such as The Fox & Hound and Rose & Thistle. She balanced both thoughts, blended them, and decided on The Hen & The Hog.

She worked out a deal with Marriott that allowed her to work remotely, and so she moved home with her mother while the renovations slogged on. People in town would stop and look and offer sympathetic smiles. "Well, I hope it works for you, honey."

The renovations took a year, and in late 2015 Patterson at last opened the doors. "People said to me, 'Nobody's coming to Halifax.' And just look around."

I did look around and would have thought I was at the most popular restaurant in Raleigh had I not spotted knick-knacks of hens and hogs. But she also aimed her finger at the window, and what she meant was for me to look beyond the room at all the storefronts lining Main. "Since I bought and started renovating, now every one of those buildings is sold, and someone is actively restoring them." I slid off my stool and stepped to the front for a better view, and when I peered out, I saw two men measuring a door frame across the street.

She soon appeared beside me and interrupted to ask what I'd like for lunch, and at first I told her no, thanks, we had another story lined up. "The shrimp and grits?" she nudged. "Barbecue and slaw on fried cornbread?" On second thought, it seemed a shame not to sample the menu. "Wedge salad with pimento cheese dressing?" she asked. I finally told her the burger would be just fine—and easier to eat in the car.

She put the order in, and I worried it might take a while because of the crowd. "We get people from all over the country," she said, though I wasn't quite sure I believed her. Maybe from a couple of counties over, *but from around the nation?*

The thought made me raise my eyes to the American flags on the second-story wall, and she must have followed my gaze. She said she'd discovered the murals decaying in the bottom of the building and had a work crew cut them out and move them upstairs. She learned air force servicemen had painted them for America's bicentennial: three flags representing 1776, 1876, and 1976. The 1976 flag was the big mural in the middle, the proud centerpiece of the whole restaurant.

I asked Patterson if she was happy, tossing the question spur of the moment; it was random, I supposed, but also a simple softball—though I anticipated a rather roundabout answer. She had traveled to almost eighty countries and given up her career to come home to a town of 234 people. She eventually retired from Marriott to run her restaurant, having no experience at all running a restaurant. Plus, she'd not only faced skeptics but also her own mortality. She moved out of her mom's house and bought one of her own that later exploded from a gas leak, fortunately when she was away.

"I am ecstatic," she said. "Best time of my life." I was surprised by her response, at how quickly she answered without hesitation, and I believed her; she said what she said with such confidence. Not only that, but her enthusiasm had apparently rippled through town and beyond. Everyone at every table seemed to be enjoying themselves and each other—and their lunch.

I hated to be eating mine out of a box, even if it was just a burger. I thanked Patterson, even hugged her, wished her continued success, and carried my take-out to the car. I couldn't resist; I dug in even before we pulled away.

Maybe it was the quality of the meat or the tasty toppings or toasted bun, or just because I was hungry, but it was the best burger I had ever sunk my teeth into.

I had to admire Patterson—and I bet Bill Marriott did, too. She hadn't just resurrected an old building or birthed a successful restaurant but had sparked an entire downtown revitalization effort, and I was beginning to think she was right, that people *were* visiting from around the country. In Halifax they could savor the entrees and learn the history both—and perhaps they would look at the North Carolina state flag in a different way.

We drove slowly through downtown, passing by those old buildings now under construction. I saw a historical marker headlined HALIFAX RESOLVES and felt something stir in *me*. I found myself cheering for Halifax and hoped tourists would as well next April 12 and every April afterward. No doubt something remarkable was happening in Halifax. Call it a stretch, but in my mind Patterson's effort had been downright revolutionary.

I took another bite of my burger and—*Oh, my gosh!* It was revolutionary, too.

CONCRETE STATUARIES

THE RUBBER BAND MAN

Stories are everywhere. Sometimes all you have to do is look out the window.

I'd set up three stories in one day near the coast: morning, noon, and afternoon. Except the middle one cancelled last minute.

When I'm on the road, I want to gather as many stories as possible because who knows when we'll be traveling that way again. It's not easy jumping from one story to the next to the next, eating out of a lunch box, and keeping them all straight in my head, but it's a good feeling to bring back a trio to add to the stockpile. Then I can spend a few days in Raleigh writing them and enjoying egg biscuits and coffee at Bojangles'.

"Must be something else we can shoot," I muttered to Robert while gazing out the window at nothing particular whizzing by. We were cruising Highway 17 in Pender County, which is not overly populated—neither the county nor the highway. It's a four-lane strip of gray-top with vast stretches of empty space. We had ninety minutes to kill, or fill, before our next shoot. *Fill,* I thought and gazed but doubted—and then spotted.

I saw an odd cluster of sculptures or statues, or something, in an otherwise empty field fifty feet off the road. It was the Cape Hatteras Lighthouse I noticed first, hundreds of miles from home, and yet this was an impressive replica. Sizeable, too; probably seventy feet tall with those familiar black-and-white stripes circling the tower in a diagonal barber-pole pattern.

I had seen many Cape Hatteras lighthouses on my travels around the state, countless copies in people's front yards, though mostly the short stubby kind and usually accompanied by ceramic seashells scattered about the lawn or plastic seagulls dangling from trees. But here was one that loomed by a lonely highway, standing upon a brick foundation, and capped with a rounded lookout just like the original. A rowboat rested nearby and beside it an anchor much too big for the boat, plus a cannon and something else, tall and rounded at the top, although by this time the odd assortment had flitted past my window, and my neck could twist only so far.

I turned back around and mulled what I'd seen, which had seemed so . . . random. The structures were just sitting there in that scraggly lot with nothing around except for the drab highway and people like me merely passing by, maybe glimpsing a quick look-see and muttering, "Hmm," but without easing off the pedal.

The road rolled on. It was early March, not really winter or spring either, a seasonal no-man's land. The trees looked like sticks—no leaves, no greenery, no pretty yellow flowers. Only the grass was yellow, the color of straw. Thin, wispy reeds leaned all along the shoulder, bowing back and forth in the wind, which gave the area a desolate, sagebrush kind of feel.

"Wonder what that was back there?"

Robert said he'd been wondering, too. "Might as well," he said and began looking for the next U-turn. And then we spotted another lighthouse.

It was a blah-colored tan, fatter and shorter than the Cape Hatteras replica but still a good forty feet tall and standing by itself on a pebbly patch of pavement close to the road. "Gotta be the same builder," Robert said and gave the pedal the heavy foot as soon as we drifted by. Now we both squinted for a U.

Highway 17 lolled ahead in one long monotonous stretch. Only a small strip shopping center on the opposite side gave us the invitation to turn, and as we pulled around, I noticed an odd-looking tree in the corner of the parking lot. A sign hung from one of its stumpy limbs. The few branches it had looked like they'd been chopped in half. I could clearly tell it wasn't a

real tree because it had no color. And growing out of the asphalt? My guess was that it was a gimmicky ad display, though a strange one, and it caught Robert's attention, too. "Gotta be the same builder," he said once again and veered into the lot.

He drove right up, and we jumped out, though I had to stand about a foot from the tree before I could read the washed-out sign that read The Eagles Nest of Hampstead. I stepped back and looked up and saw a fake eagle perched in a fake nest in a crook near the top, plus a fake squirrel frozen midcrawl on the fake tree's fake bark. I touched the bark, which was hard as rock. In fact, it *was* rock; it was concrete. And yet somebody had carved their initials on the tree inside a heart pierced by an arrow: *E.S. Loves R.S.*

Robert hauled out the camera and started shooting just in case we had a story. Then we doubled back and shot the fat lighthouse before returning to the collection we'd seen earlier.

We pulled to the side, and I peered out the window and took inventory. I counted a half dozen structures mounted in the field, including the lighthouse, boat, and anchor. *An ocean theme*, I thought. *But the cannon . . .* It looked straight out of World War II, painted army black and green, and rested between oversized wagon wheels, its gun barrel aimed directly at the highway. But rather than threatening, the cannon looked lost, as though stuck out to pasture in the shadow of the Cape Hatteras Lighthouse. And there was that other thing nearby. "What is that?" I said and pointed at a large round dome draped over a tall skinny stem. "A mushroom?"

"Toadstool." Robert had better eyes than I did, but he also wore glasses. "See the little toad on top?" I tried but couldn't make it out and turned my eyes to my watch. One hour till our next shoot.

I pushed open the car door; a gust tried to push it back. "Maybe I can find something," I said but with little confidence. I figured fat chance I'd discover the name of the builder. Robert jumped out, too, grabbed the camera, and we made our way through the weeds.

He was right. It *was* a toadstool, white as paste, with a little green toad on top, sitting like a cute puppy. I rapped my knuckles against the dome—concrete, just like the Eagles Nest tree. I picked my way to the lighthouse and knocked on it, too. Built to last. No need fretting over a hurricane.

The whole place was windswept, that wide-open field by the rushing traffic, and I pulled my coat tighter and roamed about looking and tapping and feeling as lost as everything around me. And then I saw another structure. Or were they statues? I ambled toward what appeared to be an open book resting on a pedestal as high as my chest, with two white slabs for pages. And something written on them.

I peered down at raised block letters painted black for easy reading. Built by Emmett M. Sniff, 2003–2004 at age 70 with the help of the Lord. I leaned closer to double check the spelling: *Sniff.* I giggled, and not just at the silly name but at my great good fortune. Who would have believed it? The builder's name after all, right in front of my eyes. And Sniff! With a name like that, I was sure to locate him.

Whitepages.com is a wonderful thing. I stood and grinned as I typed *Emmett M. Sniff* on my cell phone—and was shocked to see a slew of Sniffs swim onto the screen. *That many Sniffs in Pender County?* But at least Emmett topped the list. *Emmett Sniff!* I giggled and punched the number. After a few rings, an answering machine clicked on, and I explained who I was and where and left my number and hoped for a quick call back.

Phoning other Sniffs seemed like the logical next move; they had to be related. Maybe so-and-so Sniff could sniff around for Emmett Sniff. I giggled again but quit when another answering machine greeted me.

I began to think the Sniffs must be at a Sniff family reunion, because not a single Sniff I tried ever answered. I checked my watch again. We were down to our last forty minutes.

I tried to tell myself it probably wasn't a story anyway, just a bunch of random . . . *statuaries*. The word popped in my head but seemed to fit. These weren't "statues," nothing that lofty—although the lighthouse *was* awfully lofty—but more like lesser versions. And yet the concrete definitely made them weighty. *Statuaries, Sniff.* I repeated the silly words to myself, rocking with each blustery gust, and wondered what to do next.

The rusty pickup came up quick, pulled over, and hopped the curb, shaking like a dirty dog. It bounded onto the field, bouncing and jangling, kicking up dirt and dead grass, and screeched to a stop, worn black-walls biting the dust, which swirled about in a brown cloud.

The driver's door opened, and a man trotted around the hood, smiling as wide as the hood itself. He was gray-haired but balding and wore a light-colored windbreaker, his hands buried in the pockets, a thin, wiry fellow who reminded me of the wispy reeds bowing along the shoulder.

"Heard you're lookin' for me," he said in a voice as thin as his frame, high and squeaky, bordering on shrill, although he admittedly had to crank the volume because of the stubborn wind. "I'm Emmett Sniff."

I stuck out my hand and waved my other one at Robert, who looked up from the toadstool; he'd been focused on the little green toad. I told Emmett who we were. "A story for television," I said. "Did you build all these?"

He smiled and nodded, said the land was his, glad we were here, and that he'd be pleased to do an interview. "Hah, hah," he laughed. I laughed, too. *What luck!*

I positioned him with his work behind him, everything he'd built, and began by asking about the lighthouse and how much concrete went into it. "Couple truckloads. Hah!" He swayed when he laughed, boinged like a rubber band, and I could tell he was proud of those truckloads but figured he probably used somebody else's truck; I doubted his could have handled it.

"Why a toadstool?"

"I'd already built four or five them, so I just threw another one up. Hah, hah!" With his rubber-band body and animated face, Emmett Sniff was a man made for television. I asked about his unusual name. "Just like you sniff your nose," he said and spelled it. "S-N-I-F-F." I think he was proud of that, too.

He told me he'd always worked with concrete, that his father, uncle, and brother had been plasterers. Emmett had since retired but said he'd kept building anyway, just for fun. "I had most of the stuff in my head," he said and told me he hadn't used blueprints or plans for any of his creations. Although he said he once had plans to build a shopping center down the road.

"The Eagles Nest?" I asked, and he said yes but that he'd sold the property to somebody with more money than they knew what to do with who built it instead. Although he had managed to leave his own mark: the concrete tree he built in the shopping-center parking lot. I asked him about the initials on the tree.

"E.S. loves R.S. But I'm divorced from R.S. now!" This time he laughed so hard I thought he might bounce out of camera range.

I mentioned the fat lighthouse down the road, and he said that was his, too, and that he tried to make all his creations as authentic as he could. I complimented him on the cannon and told him I wouldn't have known it was fake had I not rapped on the concrete barrel. He thanked me and laughed and swayed. He boinged.

"I've enjoyed my life," he said. "I'm seventy-eight years old, in good health, and I put a lot of it to working hard, because I think that keeps you strong."

The wind gusted, which was hard on the mic, and it gave us both a moment to gaze at what he had built. I took a closer look at the concrete boat and noted the painted block letters near the bow. The boat's name read *Miss Mary Lee*, and beneath it the phrase PRAISE THE LORD. I SAW THE LIGHT.

"If you don't like what you're doing, you're not gonna do a very good job on it." This time, he didn't laugh or sway but merely smiled.

Emmett *had* done a good job, I thought, a solid job. *Solid*, I mused. *Sniff.* Only now I didn't giggle at Sniff, for here was his legacy, the work of his hands and mind. *Statuaries.* I didn't giggle at that, either.

He told me his concrete structures would be around a long time, that it took fifty years for the concrete to fully harden and another fifty to begin deteriorating. I thought about that and wondered at the vast and lonely space and guessed one day this might be prime real estate if it wasn't already. No doubt Highway 17 could use another attraction, another shopping center maybe, and if so, I hoped the builder would respect the builder before him and leave Emmett Sniff's statuaries intact.

"I've enjoyed it," he said, and the wind blew, and the reeds bowed. "Now if I could draw back about forty years, I'd start it all over again. Hah, hah, hah!"

It might have been his biggest laugh yet. His biggest boing, too.

THE SKYDIVING REPORTER

WING TIPS

"Got an idea for you."

I looked up from my desk, surprised to see the investigative reporter standing over me. He was usually digging up dirt on scandalous officials while I wandered the back roads, happily hobnobbing with country folks. We both happened to be in the newsroom that day. I eyed his suit and tie, and I bet he envied my short sleeves and khakis.

He began to tell me about his buddy at the newspaper. "He's an investigative reporter," the investigative reporter said. "But he's also a skydiver." He told me his friend had been jumping out of airplanes for forty years, that he'd just hit that milestone, and fellow jumpers were throwing an anniversary party for him. He handed me the guy's number.

"Sounds good," I said. "I'll give him a call."

He gave me an approving nod, backed away, and began striding down the narrow corridor between cubicles. I watched him go and halfway down saw him turn his head, only to lob a final thought over his shoulder. "Maybe he'd even let you jump."

The skydiver's name was Don, and he was built like a tight end on a football team. He had me by a hundred pounds and nearly a foot and would have been a hair taller had he not been going bald. He was pushing sixty.

I met him in a hangar at the Franklin County Airport in Louisburg a few days before the skydiving party. Better to run a story before the party than after, I thought.

Don told me he wrote for a publication called *Carolina Journal*; the John Locke Foundation published it. I glanced at a few of his clippings and was impressed by the hard-edged reporting.

He had also brought some memorabilia, including his college year-book. He flipped to a page and pointed to a bushy-headed kid in a washed-out photo. "You?" I said, and he smiled. He was posed with a scraggly group of fellow long hairs from a skydiving club at East Carolina University. Don told me he took his first jump on a whim at twenty and never quit.

I suggested interviewing him right there in the hangar, and Robert began setting up the camera while Don disappeared to fetch some chairs. The hangar was busy for a weekday afternoon, crawling with people clad in jumpsuits. I watched a T-shirted instructor with bulging muscles equip what looked like a shaky group of first-timers who giggled and bit their lips at the same time.

I walked around with my hands in my pockets, stepping over gear. "Sure is busy," I said to a petite woman in a sporty white jumpsuit.

"I love it," she said. "We all do. You gonna jump?"

She had lots of freckles and an adorable smile, and I was tempted to tell her, "Why not?" Instead, I shrugged and kept wandering.

In a moment, Don returned with the chairs, and I sat him down with all that action behind him.

"When I started jumping, I'd never been in an airplane," he said and showed me his log book, the first entry dated September 1971.

I could tell he was passionate about the hobby just by the way he thumbed through the log book pages. It was as if every page, every jump, had a story, and he told me several. He had jumped more than four thousand times over forty years.

I didn't want to skip over his newspaper career. I thought that was important to my story as well, though I wasn't quite sure how to link his reporting with skydiving.

"I've been involved in some pretty big stories," Don said and tapped one of the front pages. I recognized the politician flashed across it and remembered he was in prison. "You can't put someone out there in a story unless you're right." I also recognized my opportunity.

"And you can't jump out of an airplane unless you're prepared," I said.

He leaned forward, thin lips spread into a wicked smile, and looked me square in the eyes. "You can't show any fear," he said. "You just really can't show any fear."

Don didn't just report for the paper but took pictures as well, and he'd begun taking pictures when he jumped. He demonstrated for me by strapping on his skydiving helmet, which was equipped with a large camera mounted to the top and a thin wire that snaked down to his mouth. Clipped to the wire's end was a thin square he tucked between his teeth. "I press on it with my tongue," he lisped, and the camera clicked.

He said he'd snapped thousands of pictures in midair and showed me samples of skydivers posing, joining hands, even kissing while falling like bags of cement. "They're usually smiling," he said. "Just totally free."

I studied the photos and felt Don studying me, and when I glanced up, I noticed a particular gleam in his eyes along with that wicked smile again. "You gonna jump?"

I suddenly felt like one of those politicians he'd backed into a corner. And I acted like one, too. I avoided the question and looked away.

When I did, I spotted the cute little skydiver over Don's shoulder, the freckly woman who was just then strapping on a harness—the white jumpsuit looked fantastic on her. She couldn't have weighed more than a hundred pounds but was handling the gear like a pro. To me, all those straps looked heavy and complicated, and I was sure I would have tangled them into a ball.

She must have sensed me watching, because after a moment she glanced up and looked right at me and smiled—the smile looked fantastic on her, too. She held the smile, and I could see her thinking; in fact, I could feel her thinking. I knew what she was thinking. *C'mon, you can do it. It'll be soooo much fun. Jump!*

Robert and I plotted our strategy. He would remain on the ground and videotape the jumpers parachuting out of the plane, and I'd be on the plane with a hand-held mini camera, capturing the jumps from the air. What was still up in the air was me jumping from the plane. "Tell you what," Don said. We were still in the hanger, and the next thing I knew he'd grabbed an instructor to suit me up. "Just in case."

Twenty minutes later, I shuffled onto the tarmac with a dozen other jumpers, trying my best to act like a fearless reporter who'd seen it all. The harness had pushed up my trouser legs so that the cuffs of my khakis dangled at my shins, a comical case of high waters. I had also worn wing tips that day instead of my usual sneakers; I'd been thinking serious shoes for my sit-down with a serious reporter. *Anybody ever skydived wearing wing tips?* I wondered.

There were no passenger seats on the plane. They'd been replaced with two skinny parallel benches extending nose to tail, and I took a seat near one end, straddling it like everybody else. Don faced me in a solo seat against the cabin wall, and shortly after takeoff he reached over and rolled open the hatch door. A blast of cool air rushed in and kept barreling in, and just a few steps away was the open sky.

Directly behind me sat the muscle-bound instructor who'd suited me up. "If you decide to jump, we'll go tandem," he shouted over the roar. "Nothing to worry about. We'll be connected." I heard him fidgeting and then felt the straps tighten around me and his chest squeeze against my back. He'd mashed us together like a sandwich. "Remember, arms out, palms open," Muscles said, " . . . if you decide to jump."

But I wasn't thinking about jumping. I was thinking about shooting. I pressed record on the mini camera and panned the inside of the plane. I aimed it at Don, and he threw me a thumbs-up. After a while, I captured Freckles on camera, too. She raised her arm and pointed to what looked like a wristwatch. The red needle beneath the glass wavered on thirteen thousand feet.

Soon several jumpers rose and lumbered over to the open hatch, crouched, and peered at the sky beyond. The incoming air suddenly felt very heavy.

"Go!" somebody shouted, and the first jumper lunged forward, sprang from the metal lip, spread his arms, and dove. It happened so fast I wasn't sure I'd even caught it on camera; just like that, he was gone. I started to pan back to the group, but the number two jumper whooshed past me midpan, and I never saw him dive—and neither did the mini-cam; in fact, I almost dropped it. *Robert's gonna kill me*, I thought.

I did get the hang of it soon enough. Jumpers three through seven passed through the frame and into the great beyond just beautifully, Don and Freckles among them. Before jumping, they both threw me a thumbs-up. Muscles, on the other hand, gave me a shoulder clap.

"Ready?" he shouted in my ear and clapped my shoulder a second time for good measure. I'd been busy patting my own shoulder, congratulating myself on my good camera work, so that when he asked if I was ready, I answered, "Sure," without thinking.

He stood, dragging me up with him by the straps, and I quickly fumbled the camera into somebody's hands, and we shambled over to the hatch, a couple of steps away from nothing at all.

My eyes leaked from the battering wind, but Muscles thankfully slid goggles over them. "Arms out, palms open!" he shouted, and I repeated the refrain in my head, anything to occupy my mind. *Arms out, palms open . . .* I didn't want to think about what I was about to do, though I did think the air was cold, bordering on frigid. *Wish I'd brought a sweater.*

Muscles pressed his chest even tighter against my back and began rocking us like a hobby horse. He counted each time we rolled forward. "One!" *Arms out, palms open,* I thought. "Two!" *I'm really gonna do this.* "Three!" *I can't do this.* But it was too late. He burst forward, and the momentum propelled us both, spilling us over the edge and out of the plane—out, down, and away into the icy sky.

I clenched my teeth and squeezed my eyes shut as I usually do on roller-coaster rides. The air roared up at me, roared through me and all around me, suctioning my clothes to my skin, and it wasn't just loud but furious. I felt like a battered drum during a heavy-metal gig with the crazy drummer banging out the angriest cut of all in a solo jam.

"Whoooo!" Muscles screamed. "Whoooo!" I heard the thrill in his voice and peeled open my eyes.

I was surprised at what I saw below: wide, uneven squares of brown and green; surprised because everything looked so static, so harmless, even somewhat pretty. It was like I was looking at a map, and my mind flew back to geography class years ago in school when I'd studied satellite shots of earthy landscapes. Except for the rush of air, I would not have known I was hurtling toward the ground, for the ground was devoid of detail, no trees or houses, and certainly no people; I was too far up for that—but dropping fast. Don had told me a thousand feet every five seconds, a minute of free fall before the chute opened. Admiring the landscape actually put me more at ease, and it occurred to me I should make the most of the dive.

I swept my head side to side—more earthy squares—and felt surprisingly calm, insanely calm. "La de da da da . . . " I actually sang to myself. Not that the jump didn't seem real; it did. But it didn't seem—dangerous. Weird to say, free falling from thirteen thousand feet, but I couldn't wrap my mind around it. Everything was upside down and unexpected. And now my mind raced back to science class. The laws of gravity: Man falls, man lands. But I'd been falling now for almost thirty seconds with time to appreciate the view and even murmur a tune. The air, as cold and furious as it was, felt fantastically refreshing. I was glad I wasn't wearing a sweater. But I did hope I'd tied my wing tips tight enough.

Can't believe I'm doing this, I thought. *Wait till I tell Nina and the kids. But my parents—oh, they're gonna have a fit.* I thought about all of that as I fell. And I'm pretty sure I thought, *Hope the parachute opens.*

I felt another shoulder clap and craned my head just enough to see Muscles pointing his finger up. I guessed what was coming and tried to brace myself, but the hard tug that followed was so much harder than I'd imagined. With brutal force and in one fell swoop, the straps squeezed, pulled, and jerked me up and back, from horizontal to vertical in a violent half second. The breath went out of me, and then everything went quiet, immediately, as if somebody had pulled the plug on the heavy-metal jam and booted the crazy drummer off stage.

"You okay?" Muscles said; he didn't have to shout anymore. "Isn't this great?"

I was still trying to catch my breath. "Yeah," I managed, but I didn't feel great. I was already beginning to sweat; in seconds, the temperature must have shot up at least forty degrees. Not only that, but we'd started to seesaw.

"Look to your left," he said, and once again I heard the thrill in his voice. "Look at the cloud. See the rainbow?" I inventoried three clouds before I found the one with a multicolored spiral in the center. "It's the sun bouncing off the chute. Hang on, we're gonna dive right through it."

We veered hard left then straight down, and I clenched my teeth again—though more as a way to trap my breakfast in case it came flying up—and we screamed through the rainbow feet first. "Whooo!" he shouted. "Whooo!"

We finally slowed—Muscles must have been controlling us with the chute cords—and I tried to gather myself. I breathed deep and scanned the horizon, but I was sweating even more and feeling dizzy. I looked down, thinking of the patchy landscape, thinking it would help if I concentrated on something stationary, but my eyes landed on my wing tips instead, which at the time seemed good enough. I studied the scuff marks. *Need to get them polished.* Except my shoes wouldn't stay in place; they kept swaying. *Wonder if anybody's thrown up up here?*

"You okay?"

"Yeah," I said. "I am getting kinda dizzy, though."

"Six minutes and we'll be down."

Six minutes? After free falling 125 miles an hour, six minutes sounded like two hours. "Hang on," he said. "Plane coming." I glanced up just long enough to see what looked like a two-seater, eye level with us but still a good ways away. And away we went.

We plunged hard right, and my stomach lurched. "Student pilot," Muscles shouted. "Hang on," and we veered hard left. And a moment later, hard right and left again.

How he knew it was a student pilot, I had no idea, unless there were markings on the plane. I didn't bother to check; I didn't have the energy. I was spent. I drooled, and somebody below may have felt a few odd raindrops fall from the sunny sky.

"Gonna let him land," Muscles said, which meant dillydallying even more. A moment earlier we'd been plummeting. Now I was so light-headed I was scared I might pass out—and scared, too, of ending up in Don's newspaper: REPORTER IS SKYDIVING CASUALTY.

"Here we go!" The shout brought me out of it, and so did our next move. We shot toward the ground like a bullet.

Down we dove, and up stormed my stomach into my throat. The ground came at me fast, now whirring with detail: houses, airport, grass, landing strip.

"Legs up!" We slowed suddenly, as if the air had broken our fall, had caught us and held us, but with a loose grip. We were slipping, still falling, and faster than I wanted to—even though I wanted my feet fast on the ground.

My heels touched first, rear end a close second, and I went skidding along the grass. I'm sure the skid would have been longer and rougher had Muscles not put on the foot brakes, too. For the most part, the touchdown was smooth.

The parachute collapsed around us, and I slumped forward and dropped my chin to my chest. I was exhausted, hot, dizzy—and on television.

I heard commotion and pulled my head up to see three cameras in my face. Robert, Don, and another jumper were pointing their lenses at me. "How was it?" somebody cried. I tried to summon a grin and play to the cameras even in my condition. "Whooo," I said, borrowing a line I'd heard too many times, though mine was a far wimpier version. "That was great."

I saw Don pull his eye out of the viewfinder and cock his head. He seemed to be studying me; the investigator in him must have sensed I was lying. He dropped his camera, grabbed my arm, and helped me up, while Muscles freed me of the harness. "You don't look so good," Don murmured, quiet enough so that the microphones didn't pick it up.

He began dragging me to the terminal, a tight end pulling dead weight. I told him I could use some water. I did not tell him my stomach might need a toilet, but I think he'd figured that out, too.

He seemed good-natured about it all—maybe too good. I looked at him at one point, and there was that smile of his, that wicked smile. He saw me looking, and I'm sure he knew I was wondering, *Why the smile?*—the man was one keen reporter. He kept me waiting a beat but at last revealed his secret.

"At least your wing tips made it."

POSTSCRIPT

I don't like showing off in a story. Some reporters love it. News directors, too. They want their reporters seen on scene, want them to walk and talk, show and tell, wield a prop for the camera, and point and gesture. Eager-to-please reporters are happy to ham it up.

I looked long and hard at the video of me parachuting to earth. "Oh, we gotta use it," Robert said. It had been a few days since the jump, and he had begun to edit the story.

"But I look like I'm gonna throw up," I said. In fact, I still felt dizzy and could barely stand to keep my eyes on the video. I felt sick watching me feel sick.

It was Robert who urged me to call the doctor. "Just to be safe." I think he was also sick—of me hovering over him while he edited.

I told the doctor my skydiving story while sitting on the exam-room table and chuckled all the way through it, convinced the dizziness was all in my head. I was still grinning when he pulled a pointy instrument out of my ear and frowned. "It's bleeding," he said.

"What?"

"Must have been the pressure from the fall. Your ear is bleeding."

He said it probably wasn't serious, but to make sure, he gave me a hearing test, which I passed. "Should clear up on its own in a couple of weeks."

I went back to the station, a bit dazed at the diagnosis, and informed Robert, who seemed concerned but also distracted. He had pulled up the story again on his computer, having left the ending unfinished, and there I was, sitting on the grass, Muscles behind me, parachute around me, my face as white as the clouds we'd plunged through. Robert was gung-ho on using it. "The perfect ending," he said. "Don't worry. People are gonna love it."

I was sure the news director would love it. And Muscles, Freckles, and Don. They'd all throw me a thumbs-up, I was sure. I supposed I was proud of myself as well, despite everything, bleeding ear and all.

I watched the story when it aired. I listened to Don's articulate interview, admired my camera work inside the plane—minus the herky-jerky moves, which were wisely edited out—and I thought Robert's video from the ground looked spectacular, especially seeing those ballooning parachutes: big, bright, and colorful.

I admit I winced as the story wound down, when I saw Muscles and me winding down, landing, and skidding to a stop. "Whooo. That was great," I said on television.

I grinned watching myself. I grinned because my face didn't look quite so pale. The new color-enhancement option on the editing machine had worked wonders—that was a secret I was pretty sure Don would never dig up.

I smiled; despite it all, I did. My ear was much better by then; the dizziness had finally subsided. When the story ended, I allowed myself not just a pat on the shoulder but—what the heck—a good solid clap.

Thirteen thousand feet, I mused. *I did it!*

And so did my wing tips.

ANDREWS GEYSER

HIGHEST SPOUT IN THE WORLD!

"Mystical" is how I'd describe it.

I had seen photos of Andrews Geyser, a fountain that shot water two hundred feet high. So powerful was its trajectory that the water formed a solid beam on its way up, then finally ran out of gas, curled, and rained down. Except there was no gas. No electricity, either.

Andrews Geyser was a purely natural phenomenon with a little man-made help. It was near the town of Old Fort in McDowell County, on the way to Asheville. I admired a picture of it I'd seen on a postcard, that towering stream of water. The base of the fountain was intriguing as well, a concrete pentagon with ornate curlicues at each corner, and surrounding the base was rich green grass, so green the postcard people had probably doctored it. Indeed, the picture looked too good to be true. And it was.

The geyser was busted. No water, no story. We were driving through Old Fort anyway, so we stopped for its other tourist attraction: a giant arrowhead in the middle of town. An arrowhead usually fits in the palm of a hand, but this was thirty feet tall and chiseled from solid granite. It stood high on a pedestal next to the Chamber of Commerce and was erected in 1930 as a symbol of peace between early pioneers and Native Americans.

If the fountain wouldn't do, this would—how rare, a small town with two unusual landmarks. For now, our viewers would know of just one.

The arrowhead was impressive, except that it didn't move. It was simply mounted, sharp end pointed at the sky, and so our video was static. Robert did the best he could, and when we finally packed up, I thought I had a pretty good story. But I also suspected there was a better story, if only the fountain wasn't busted.

I checked on it once or twice in the months that followed, but the geyser was either still broken or the person from the Chamber of Commerce didn't know, which was understandable. It was a ways away, a fifteen-minute drive from the center of town. After a while, I wrote it off and stopped calling and checking.

Until 2018, when I was planning to head to McDowell County for a railroad story. Marion, North Carolina, is the county seat, just east of Old Fort, and I'd heard the mayor of Marion, Steve Little, was the main man to talk to about trains.

His excitement sizzled across the phone line. He was probably older than I was but sounded like a very smart child, one who poured over books in the library and couldn't wait to tell his mom what he found. He told me he'd even performed railroad stories by dressing in costume and acting in front of audiences, which made sense given his manner of speech. He spoke clearly, enunciated his words, and was full of oomph and flair even in our casual conversation.

Somewhere in our railroad talk, the fountain bubbled to the surface. "But is the fountain working?" I asked.

"Yes," he said, "oh, yes."

He told me it had been repaired and was as passionate about the fountain as he was about the railroad. He even offered to take me to it. "You'll get some great pictures," he said, which I was happy to hear after the arrowhead.

A couple of weeks later, Robert and I were following Mayor Little along narrow roads that wound through areas thick with brush, past weathered barns and rusty mobile homes, and I wondered if anyone dared live in them or even ventured out this far.

And yet there were signs pointing THIS WAY TO THE ANDREWS GEYSER. And there it was at last. It *was* true; the postcard had done it justice. Well, except for the grass; it wasn't so green. But the area did possess a mystical quality—mystical to me, I supposed, because I could hardly believe what I was seeing. For so long, I had thought of the fountain as dead in the water, but here it was in all its majesty, shooting a powerful stream sky high. "Probably the most unique fountain in the United States," said Steve.

The mayor had probably seen the fountain in person a hundred times, or a thousand, but I could tell he was still in awe of it. So was I. We both stood and stared while Robert powered up and shot—the pictures were irresistibly good.

We eventually sat on a park bench fifty feet from the spray. It was breezy that morning, and though in awe of the fountain, I was glad for the distance. The day was also cool and crisp, early March, which gave the area a lonely aura. We were in a wide-open space, having walked several stone steps down onto the grass, so it was like we were in a shallow bowl framed by dense woods. The fountain was the centerpiece; it continually *whooshed*, and the sound was both soothing and chilling at the same time.

I shivered beneath a much-too-thin coat. Steve wore a down jacket and wool sailor cap, and I had a feeling he was plenty warm; his face glowed. "You drive through a lot of beautiful, undeveloped woodland just to get here," he said, eyes twinkling.

He was a man with many titles, and it wasn't long before I learned of the adjectives attached to them: Informed Town Mayor, Passionate Historian, Enthusiastic Performer.

"It links back to the construction of the railroad," he said—Railroad Historian was another title. "Without the railroad, there would be no Andrews Geyser."

It had been daunting to build a railroad in the mountains, but the state succeeded, and in the 1870s, trains began chugging by McDowell County, thanks in large part to a man named Major James W. Wilson. Steve's rosy face turned rosier when he mentioned him. He told me Wilson had long been his hero.

Wilson was an engineer—and, perhaps, a marketing genius. "Major Wilson built a five-story hotel," Steve said, his voice an octave higher. It had once stood just a few feet from where we were sitting. "It had the largest dining room in the state west of Greensboro." Steve smiled and gave the picnic table a satisfying pat.

The hotel opened in 1884. Trains would stop, and people would visit

the grand hotel, eat lunch in the great dining room, and even spend the night before catching the next train and continuing their journey. Sometimes they continued on to Asheville, which also boasted of grand hotels and fine dining rooms. And sometimes they did *not* bother to stop at Major Wilson's hotel because of what awaited them down the track.

"So Major Wilson thought, 'What can I do to make my hotel a destination spot?'" Steve drummed his fingers, and I realized he'd slipped into his actor role, playing the part of the genius Major Wilson. "'I'm going to create a fountain!'" he said, his voice nearly as high as the fountain Wilson wound up creating. "'The highest spout in the world!'"

Steve said Wilson dammed up a nearby stream to form a pond then ran an iron pipe from the pond under the railroad tracks all the way down to the bowl, a distance of two miles and an elevation difference of five hundred feet. He fitted the end of the pipe with a half-inch nozzle, pointed it toward the sky, and let gravity do the rest. "And the water shot up in the air just by the force of pressure, the pressure of water reaching its own level. It was an incredible sight to see."

Wilson proudly posted a sign that read WORLD'S TALLEST FOUNTAIN. Steve wrote the message across the air with his finger. "And that just captivated everybody's attention, that magical fountain with this gigantic plume shooting two hundred feet in the air, and people would say, 'I want to go where the fountain is.'"

Steve was a picture of animation between his active hands and rosy face. Rarely had I interviewed anyone better. But something nagged at me, and I had to butt in. I asked him why the Andrews Geyser wasn't called the Wilson Geyser; after all, Wilson had been the one who'd built it. Steve shook his head and launched into the next part of his story.

It was Wilson who'd been charged with extending the railroad west from Old Fort to Asheville. His team had blasted their way through granite using nitroglycerin, the first time nitro had ever been used in the southeast. Most of the workers were convicts from the penitentiary in Raleigh. They built seven tunnels through the mountains and opened western North Carolina to the rest of the state in what had been a heroic feat of engineering.

Then came Wilson's grand hotel and awe-inspiring fountain. But in 1903 the hotel burned.

"Wilson's hotel?" I said.

Steve nodded and told me it burned to the ground. "And there was no one to look after the fountain, and after a couple of years it fell into disrepair and became covered in vines and bushes." He shook his head. "Sad."

Sadder still, I thought, was the fate of poor Wilson. I learned he died a few years later, his hotel gone and his fountain in ruins.

But Steve was far from finished. He began to tell me about George Fisher Baker. "Probably the third wealthiest man in the United States. Well, he's going to do something about it." Steve banged the picnic table with his fist, and I had to admit, I was glad to see him riled up again after Wilson's death and the fountain's demise. "He's going to replace it. But we're not going to call it a fountain. We're going to call it a geyser!" He grinned and punched both *geyser* and the table, and I realized he was now playing the role of Baker. "And George Fisher Baker said, 'My friend, Colonel Andrews, never got recognition.'"

Steve—and the actor Steve—laid out what happened next. Baker paid for the geyser and acquired the naming rights. He named it for Andrews, a railroad executive who'd also been instrumental in extending the rail lines west. "But interestingly, Andrews had nothing to do with the railroad here," Steve said with a mischievous grin, as though he knew something other historians didn't. I think he knew the geyser should have been named for Wilson.

But he gave Baker credit for rebuilding the broken fountain. "When it came back online, it was every bit as high as before. I've seen pictures that will knock your socks off," he said, and I thought of the postcard I'd seen and the two-hundred-foot-high tower of water.

Baker did not rebuild the hotel, only the fountain, and the fountain kept rail passengers riveted to the windows.

But progress is a funny thing; it keeps progressing. Eventually, the journey west became rather routine and not altogether profitable. So in 1972, Southern Railway halted passenger service through the area, and when the railroad stopped, the water did, too. There was no use maintaining the geyser.

"Well, I was in law school at Wake Forest at the time," Steve said, hands folded in front of him. "And I went down to the courthouse." I sensed he was playing another role, that of his younger self. "I knew how to search a title, so I thought, 'I just want to see who owns that now.' Well, I looked, and I found the deed. Southern Railway still owned it."

His rising voice signaled his surprise. "The covenant of title said, 'I'm giving this to you, together with the obligation that you're going to maintain it in perpetuity as a memorial to Col. Alexander B. Andrews.'"

George Fisher Baker had written the covenant, which Southern Railway had accepted. "The covenant in the deed says you have to maintain it," Steve said, and pointed his finger at me—I think he wanted me to play the role of Southern Railway.

The much younger Steve, meanwhile, had pointed his finger at a powerful company and wrote the company a letter, which Southern Railway abruptly brushed off. "'Regretfully, we think the geyser has just served its time,'" Steve said, quoting the railway's ho-hum response.

"Wrong answer!" He punched the air with his fist. "Hold on, you can't do that! The covenant! You have to maintain it!"

Through the mail went more letters, dashed back and forth, until Southern Railway realized it could no longer ignore the evidence. It had no desire whatsoever to spend money rebuilding the fountain, plus more money maintaining it—in perpetuity, no less. The only out, it seemed, was to deed the geyser to Old Fort and let the town take care of it.

"The town is going to accept it and get it fixed up. 'And we're going to make this a city park and restore it to its former beauty.'" Now Steve was playing the mayor of Old Fort from the mid-1970s. "But, oh my goodness," he said, "the pond that's been the water source has filled up with silt."

The fountain had been shuttered for two years. "Terribly overgrown," Steve said. So he and other volunteers jumped in, dredged the silt, cleared the brush, worked on the fountain, and got it going again. The water spouted less than half as high as before—the age of the pipes, perhaps—but that did nothing to dampen people's spirits. Even an eighty-foot torrent was awe inspiring.

Old Fort rededicated the geyser in 1976, the same year America celebrated its bicentennial. "They invited me to be one of the speakers," Steve said, grinning like a giddy schoolkid. "I was so excited. I even had me a three-piece suit." I could feel his excitement, even forty years later across a picnic table. The geyser had spouted water ever since, except for occasional breakdowns.

"It draws people from all over the place, and it's just amazing. You don't hear the hum of an engine because there's not an engine running it. It's just nature. No artificial anything."

Now it was my turn to lean across the table and fold my hands. Time for my role, me the reporter seeking the big picture. "What's the moral of the story?"

"The moral is don't give up. Just keep on trying."

"It's a story of the little guy against the big guy," I said.

Steve leaned across the table, too, and in his final act on camera, theatrically delivered the last line.

"I slayed a dragon."

He was talking about Southern Railway, of course. A dragon breathes fire, and Steve had fought it with water; in this case, water was the mystical element.

Mystical . . . I turned to the geyser once again and admired the natural power of its propulsion. I followed the trajectory all the way to the top, and when my eyes reached the apex, I thought, curiously, of the arrowhead back in town, that thirty-foot arrowhead, also piercing the sky. Old Fort was indeed blessed with two towering landmarks, each distinct in their own way.

But the area was also fortunate, I thought, to have a man like Steve, for he provided a voice for local history—and a loud voice. What a passionate historian he was.

And what a fine actor, too.

THE SERPENTARIUM

SNAKES AND SINATRA

I almost fainted.

We'd been in Wilmington shooting a story at the Museum of the Bizarre, and I was fine with skeleton heads and the serial killer's knife collection. But then the curator said, "Hey, you might find another story next door. The Serpentarium."

I had noticed it when we parked, the tall L-shaped brick building with a poster draped over the top that read "Deadly Snakes." But what really gave me goosebumps was a banner jutting from the edge of the L that showed a snake, not on its belly but in raised, ready-to-pounce position. I have long had a snake phobia, so I stayed well clear of the place. I was far more comfortable with the macabre.

But toward the end of our visit, the man at the Museum of the Bizarre mentioned the man at the serpentarium—and what a bizarre story. So when I was done, I did my best to swallow my fear—some snakes can swallow a whole rabbit—and walked next door to check it out.

It was as hot as a greenhouse when I entered and the air just as stagnant. And the smell: putrid, moldy. I thought of dead skin and the serial killer's knife collection.

The man at the desk told me the serpentarium owner wasn't there. "But you're free to look around." I don't know what possessed me to do so, to look around, unless the shrunken head had possessed me, the one at the museum with the voodoo spell on it.

I shuffled beyond the lobby into what looked like a cave where the smell grew stronger along with my loathing. There were snakes everywhere: long, fat, spotted, hooded, snakes with skinny heads, fat heads, and many flicking their forked tongues—those horrifying tongues.

The snakes were behind glass, but I could practically feel them slithering up my spine, curling around my neck, flicking the side of my face. I shivered despite the stale air and looked away and tried to hurry through, but the lights were low and display cases here and there, so it was a bit of a maze, and I was feeling dizzy. I almost put out a hand to steady myself, but then my hand would have been a mere pane away from a snake, and I didn't trust either one, even if the glass had been a yard thick and the snake just a foot long.

I finally stumbled out in a sweat and lurched across the street to where Robert was waiting. He'd been finishing up at the museum, grabbing a few last shots of the bizarre, and said something about my face looking as pale as the car; the station owned a fleet of SUVs in "Glacier White." I told him he might have to shoot the serpentarium story by himself whenever we returned. He shrugged. "No problem," he said and started the car.

"Crank the AC," I croaked.

Snakes shed their skin, and in time I shed my fear. Months had passed since my quick visit to the Cape Fear Serpentarium, and I'd convinced myself it wasn't that bad. I was also lured by the story, a good story, I was sure. I remembered what the man at the Museum of the Bizarre had told me about the owner, so I stocked myself full of confidence and bravado, and I called him.

Dean Ripa was a man with a deep voice who did not sound impressed. He said he had welcomed television crews before and was used to the drill but, okay, he said, anytime. We picked a date, and I hung up and told Robert we'd both go. He looked at me sideways. "You sure?"

"No problem."

"Conceivably, the most dangerous snake in the world," Dean said, and my legs quivered. I hoped he hadn't noticed, that he was busy watching the snake, making sure the case was shut tight and locked.

He had started the tour with the deadliest, and my phobia struck like a King Cobra, which at that moment flared up and stared right through me. It had black beady eyes and a face that seemed patched together with tiles. "The only snake known to kill elephants," Dean said.

I was struck both by the snake—though not literally struck—and by Dean. He seemed unusually laid back, as though he'd just climbed out of bed to meet us. He had bed-head hair and leaned on a wooden walking stick, not that he needed the support. He was younger than I was, tall and thin with a black goatee. I could have used the stick myself; I was rubbery all over, but when he wasn't lazy and leaning, he used it like a teacher tapping the blackboard.

He tapped on the Gaboon Viper case next, and I could barely stand to look. And yet I was standing a bit straighter, not that the Gaboon didn't look as ominous as the Cobra, but it was just so—I supposed I was standing in judgment—just so ugly. It reminded me of a dead fish, white as a cod's belly and wide as a flounder.

"The largest head of any viper and has the largest fangs and the most venom of any viper," Dean said and pointed at the five skulls and cross-bones below the glass, little red stickers lined in a row. A ranking system, he said. The Gaboon was so lethal it earned five out of five. "The bite is agonizing and deadly," read the accompanying caption. But if ranked for good looks, I would have left the case sticker free.

I was starting to feel better, my attention diverted away from the danger and focused on Dean. He had lived an adventurous life, despite his laid-back manner. "I've been to about thirty-five countries," he said. "I'd usually go into a small village in the middle of some remote area and live with the native people." Then he would scour the jungle searching for snakes. Although he told me he'd backed off in recent years because he had a family now. In fact, he said he lived with his family in an apartment above the serpentarium. I raised my eyes and wondered how well his wife slept.

He talked about tracking a mamba snake and showed me one, a live one. It was yellowy-green with big, dark, alien eyes. "You might have to climb 150 feet in the air to catch it. If you don't fall and break your neck, the mamba will get you," he laughed.

He moved to another case and pointed to a snake from Australia called the Inland Taipan. "The tiniest drop of venom that would fit on the head of a pin will kill you." He pulled a ring of keys from his pocket, fit one into the lock—and began opening the case.

Robert and I stepped back but not Dean. He opened it wide and propped the window on a dowel, and to my astonishment the Inland was soon outbound. It slithered partway over the threshold, flicked its tongue, and poked its head toward the floor. It had a small head, its body the color of a worn penny, and I remember thinking it didn't look all that poisonous. My bravado had returned—sometimes reporters feel immune to danger. I also figured Dean knew what he was doing. He had opened the case so Robert didn't have to fight the glare of the glass. Smart man. "Does it make you nervous being near it?" I asked. He replied with another laugh.

We watched it for a while, draped over the edge of the case, its head just a foot or two above the carpet, tongue flicking. Then Dean finally wielded his stick. He hooked the snake, which curled around it, and pushed the Inland in, then closed the case and locked it.

"I've been bitten fourteen times, you see, by venomous snakes," he said—maybe he thought he was immune, too. He told me he should have been dead already, especially the time the Bushmaster nabbed him. "Plunged the fangs deep into the muscle of my forearm."

I asked how it happened, where he was. "In the jungle?"

"No," he said. "Right here," and pointed to the next case, and how I wished he'd had a better story. "Careless," he said.

The Bushmaster had the looks to match its ominous name. Its head was as black and crispy as a charcoal briquette repeatedly torched on the backyard grill. "I mean, what was your immediate thought?" I asked.

"Well, that I was gonna die," he said in a nonchalant way as though the answer was obvious. Immediate injections of antivenom saved him. He said he kept some handy, which I suppose should have been obvious, too.

He told me he'd been fascinated by snakes even as a boy and had eventually become internationally known for them, for breeding them and capturing some of the rarest, deadliest snakes in the world. But he also had another talent. He could sing.

Here was the twist to his story, what the man at the Museum of the Bizarre had told me. Dean Ripa had been the front man for the famous Tommy Dorsey Orchestra from 2001 to 2006. Back at the station after that first trip, still wrestling with my phobia, I had sampled his singing online and thought he sounded just like Frank Sinatra. I even picked out a tune I knew we just had to use if we did a story. I could see it in my mind: shots of those deadly slithering snakes while the song played. Dean Ripa, sounding just like Frank Sinatra, singing, "I like you under my skin." It was that song, that strange career twist, that had convinced me to go back to the serpentarium.

Now here I was, and I brought it up at last. "Have you always had a good singing voice?" He told me he had, that he'd enjoyed that time in his life; but all that, he said, was in the past. He'd given it up for the snakes with no regrets, even after fourteen potentially fatal snake bites. "And you keep doing it," I said.

He laughed. "Well, yeah, it's too late to stop."

He showed us other cases, one with Daisy, the man-eating crocodile— the serpentarium displayed more than just serpents—and another with a giant snapping turtle, its head looking as heavy as a blacksmith's anvil. "Powerful beacon jaws. He can bite your fingers off with ease. He can break a broomstick in half."

"What's his name?"

"Chomp." This time he didn't laugh, but I did.

We spent two hours at the serpentarium, and I was rather proud of myself. I felt pretty good, not wobbly-legged at all. My passion for the story had apparently conquered my fear of the snakes, though I had my doubts whether it had done so permanently. Snake skin might be easier to shed than snake phobia. I didn't see myself returning again.

But I was leaving on a high note—or on a melodious note anyway. Maybe my legs *were* a little wobbly, the joints springy. I found myself skipping across the street to the car, thinking of the unique story I had bagged. I hadn't done anything as daring as Dean, hadn't climbed a tree in the jungle and netted a mamba, but I had stared my phobia in its beady-eyed face and come away with a prize.

My skip became a little dance, jiggly legs and all, and I did my best Frank Sinatra. "I like you under my skin . . ."

My best Dean Ripa.

POSTSCRIPT

Dean Ripa's life came to a terrible, tragic end. He did not die of a snake bite.

Two months after I interviewed him, Dean's wife shot him in the head in the apartment they shared above the serpentarium. Regina Ripa was charged with first-degree murder and sent to jail.

The serpentarium struggled to stay open but closed permanently one year later, in 2018, and the snakes were sold. I suspect Dean would have been upset by that, his life's work suddenly gone—poof. Or maybe he would have been nonchalant—easy come, easy go. He lived every day with danger, side-by-side with jaws of death, and seemed nonchalant about that, too. Of course, he was careful; he knew how quick those snakes could pounce. But in the end, I suppose, he never saw it coming.

Nor guessed who would deliver the fatal blow.

HOOTIE AND GENE

There are stories where everything goes right. And where everything goes wrong.

Charles Kuralt knew something about the wrong end of a story. He was that illustrious wanderer for CBS News who captured apple-pie slices of small-town America, including the adorable animals of America. But he once said that of every animal story he ever did, the critters were always running away from the camera. Kuralt was convinced they hated cameras, or the sounds of cameras, and his stories inevitably came to the same disappointing end—the rear end.

So I was pretty sure my story on a wild owl was doomed from the start. I'd heard of a man from Wendell who put his boat in every evening at dusk and took it all the way to the end of the lake where a barred owl greeted him from a tree. Then the man—Gene was his name—would hold out his hand and offer it a little fish, which the owl would swoop down and snatch, practically from out of Gene's palm. Then it would fly back to its branch, and the scene would soon repeat. Gene had named his feathery friend and written a children's book about him full of vivid pictures he'd taken himself. The book was called *My Friend Hootie*.

It sounded like a promising story, which is what led me to Wendell. And yet the whole way there I thought of Kuralt. I thought no way we'd find an owl, no matter how many times Gene had assured me on the phone that, yes, Hootie would be waiting for us on his branch just like always. But I remained doubtful and kept second-guessing my decision to make the trip. I thought that even if Hootie *was* there, he'd fly away as soon as we came into view.

Wendell is twenty minutes or so from Raleigh, not too far, but the workday was already over; it was after six. I figured we'd have to fiddle with the boat, the motor, the life jackets before even beginning to putter all the way to the end of the lake. Gene had told me it covered 167 acres, and I was betting there were plenty of No Wake signs along the way. I had a feeling we were in for a long, slow ride, and it was all a big gamble.

When we finally arrived at the boathouse, the first part went just the way I thought—lots of fiddling, followed by monotonous puttering, although I will say the lake was certainly pretty and Gene was nice to talk to over the hum of the motor. He told me he'd grown up at Lake Wendell and had always loved the outdoors. "Since I was born," he said.

He became a biologist and professor at North Carolina State then worked in Washington as a top administrator at the US Department of Interior for twenty-five years, helping to shape federal wildlife policy. Now he was retired and well into his eighties.

"Ten years ago in the spring is when I first called him, and he came as a young owl," Gene said and told me he and Hootie had bonded almost immediately; of course, the fish he fed him helped. Then there was the time Gene was farther up the lake, far from Hootie's usual perch. "And I looked up, and there's ol' Hoot right over my head, and when he saw that I recognized him, he turned and went right back to that perch and waited for me to bring the fish. And I sat there thinking, Who's training who here now?" We both shared a good laugh.

The sun was low in the sky by the time Gene finally slowed the engine. We crept between cypress trees with mossy canopies; the end of the lake was more of a swamp, and I found it a little haunting, especially when Gene cut the engine another notch and kept his voice low. "Getting close," he said. "Around that last tree. Almost there."

I felt the hair on my neck rise, along with my hopes. We dribbled up to the last cypress, and the moss closed in, so heavy it blocked the view on the other side. I couldn't see, even when I risked craning my head, careful not to rock the boat or make a sound. There *was* no sound. Gene had cut the engine, and we drifted, black water below, mossy blanket above, closer . . . closer . . .

"There he is," Gene said, jarring me upright—I did rock the boat. "Just like clockwork." My eyes swept the trees. There were so many, the area dense, and it took me a moment to find him; but there he was, perched high, chest out, big and feathery, feathers brown and white, eyes black and wide. I was shocked to see him but managed to remain still. Hootie didn't move, either, but I could tell he was watching us and feared he might eye the big eye in the boat, the one with a lens and a zoom—and if he did, Hootie might zoom.

"Hey there, ol' Hoot," Gene called as we bumped onto a small patch of earth beneath his tree. "That's his feeding perch. When he wants a fish, that's where he sits, right there on that limb." Gene fished a fish from his fishing pail, and now Hootie did move. He rotated his head sideways and down in one smooth motion, as if on greased ball bearings. The little fish was alive, flopping about in Gene's palm, and that's when Gene told Robert to make a move for his video camera. "Nice and slow." I tried not to breathe as Robert wrestled it onto his shoulder, the Sony like a cinder block, but Hootie stayed put, even when the red light blinked on and the battery purred.

"Are you ready, buddy? Are you ready?" Gene called. Hootie stared. "He seems to be as eager to see me as much as I am to see him." It occurred to me that Gene suddenly seemed much younger than his eighty-plus years. He bounced the little fish in his hand. "You ready, Hoot?" I almost didn't want him to toss it; I was getting good sound— "Ready, buddy?"—and Robert's camera was trained on Hootie, who was cooperating nicely. "He's even smiling for you."

Gene gave the fish a final

bounce and tossed it below the tree. It took only a second or two before Hootie flailed his wings, swept down, and thumped in front of the fish, which he promptly snagged with a claw and carried back to the branch. It had all happened less than fifteen feet from us, though it had happened quickly. Robert kept mum, but I was sure he was thinking he'd like a few more swoop-downs to shoot. Fortunately, Gene's pail was full of wiggling bait.

"He's putting on a show for you," he said after touchdown number two. "Hootie enjoys it as much as I do," he said after touchdown three. I was enjoying it myself and thinking Kuralt would have been amazed. Each time Hootie landed, he hesitated just a moment before clutching the fish and flying back, and during that hesitation, he pointed those big eyes directly at us while Robert aimed the camera directly at him. We couldn't have asked for a better close-up. But it was still oh-so-quick. Two or three seconds later, and Hootie was flying back to the branch to enjoy his meal, which instantly vanished.

The fish were barely bigger than minnows, appetizers really, but still, I worried Hootie was getting full and might stop flying toward us off his perch. I worried whether we had enough video—a television crew always wants more—and I hoped Hootie wanted more, too. Gene tossed another fish.

Maybe he *was* full. Or maybe he was angry at yet another itty-bitty appetizer, debating whether he even wanted to bother. In any case, Hootie stood by the flopping fish without taking it—seven, eight, nine, ten seconds, those big eyes staring alternately at the fish and at the eye on Robert's shoulder. I imagined Robert's eyes had grown even bigger than Hootie's. What an astounding close-up, a wild owl filling the lens. Gene seemed impressed, too. "He's putting on a show for you."

At last Hootie snatched the fish and this time did not fly back to his branch but rather sailed off through the cypress trees and was gone. Robert pulled his eye from the viewfinder and gave me a thumbs-up; he'd captured what would almost certainly be the closing shot of our story.

"That's it," said Gene, who obviously knew the routine. "That's all for tonight." But it had been enough. It had been beautiful. "Can't get much better than that."

We pulled away from the tree, Gene powered up the engine, and we made our way back to the boathouse. That long, slow ride, now nearly full dark, was ever so peaceful. I leaned back and listened to the gentle rush of water and thought of Kuralt, my hero Kuralt, and how he would have loved this. He loved nature and a good story, and I thought how envious he would be. I had the complete package, a peaceful setting and a wonderful story with a beautiful end.

Not a rear end.

CHEWY

FAITHFUL FRIEND

I had no idea how a dog could possibly ride a motorcycle.

Of course, it couldn't steer one, but would it plant its front paws on the driver's shoulders, wrap its hind legs around the driver's waist? I had trouble seeing it in my head. And what about its head? Did the dog wear a helmet? I was curious—curiosity killed the cat—and I was worried about the dog, too.

Somebody had told me about its motorcycle adventures. But they also said the dog wasn't doing so well, still riding but . . . "Better get on it quick." I called the dog's owner.

Butch was soft-spoken. He said he and Chewy had traveled all over the country. "Chewy?" I said. I liked the story already. Even more when Butch told me about all the fallen veterans the two of them had honored. Butch was a veteran himself and said he and Chewy had become part of a motorcycle contingent, grateful and proud to pay their respects at military funerals.

But Chewy . . . the motorcycle . . . I started to ask how that worked, how he rode, the way he sat, but Butch stopped me. "Good days and bad days," he said, "and he's been having some bad days lately. Maybe in a couple weeks. Can you call back?"

That didn't sound so good, and Butch's soft voice made it sound even worse. It was. "Cancer," he said, and I offered my sympathies. "But he's a fighter," he added, which was good to hear. "Maybe later."

I hung up, holding onto hope but also feeling like it might be too late. I hadn't even met Chewy and I liked him already. He and Butch sounded like a good team. I admired them for honoring those fallen vets. I loved the name Chewy. And Chewy on a motorcycle . . . ? I still wondered how that worked.

A few weeks went by. Robert and I were shooting stories all over the state, and I didn't want to impose on Butch. I figured I'd give him more time—and Chewy, too. Time heals. Maybe Chewy's condition had improved. Or, I feared, perhaps it was the other way around. Maybe Butch was the one who now needed time to heal.

I dreaded the follow-up call but punched the numbers anyway, and when Butch answered, I think my voice was softer than his was the first time. But to my surprise, his was much louder than before. Chewy was doing better, he said. His little buddy kept bouncing back. Butch was still concerned, told me he didn't want to tire Chewy out, but, yes, he said, a story would be fine, and he suggested the day.

I'd been tiring *myself* out. Too much traveling, too many stories, so many deadlines. The day he picked was already crammed, but this was my chance. I cradled the phone and drummed my pencil on my desktop calendar, squinted at what I'd scribbled on that day's date, and squeezed a tiny bit more lead in the bottom corner of the square.

I asked Butch if the two of them could come to the television station late in the day. I would interview him in the WRAL azalea gardens next to the building. Then we'd capture them riding up and down Centennial Parkway just a stone's throw away. But even as I laid out the plan, I thought how lazy it sounded. People knew those famous gardens; thousands of folks had toured them over the years. Many knew Centennial Parkway; North Carolina State's second campus was tucked back from the road. When our story

aired, I was sure viewers would recognize the setting and know I had opted for the easy route. They'd realize I had simply stepped outside the station doors. Much too convenient—but so little time.

Butch said the plan sounded good; I doubted my concerns were obvious to him. What probably was obvious was when I told him to make sure to bring the motorcycle.

———

Chewy was a border collie mix with fluffy gold-and-white fur. He was a good-sized dog, around fifty-five pounds, thirteen years old. I could see his age in his face. He squinted even though it was cloudy that day and cool, early January 2016. But the squint and his prominent nose, typical of the breed, gave him a wise, majestic look, like an elder statesman of dogs.

Butch gave me the basics in the gardens, squatting on one knee while petting his furry friend who sat quietly. He said he'd rescued him just before Chewy turned two.

I heard "rescued" and straightened; I was squatting on one knee, too. Butch told me he'd found Chewy at the SPCA. "He was way underweight and very afraid of people." But curiously, not of Butch. The dog kept circling his legs at the time. "And I just dropped to my knees and talked with him and decided, 'You're going home.'" Chewy had been at the shelter three days. It was overcrowded, and the staff had already planned to put him down.

On his first night at his new home, Chewy chewed up the window shades in the master bathroom and later—ruhro!—chewed Butch's shoe. "And he got his name Chewy," Butch said, grinning. He was also a smart dog who quickly learned right from wrong.

A few years went by. Butch's wife was a cancer survivor who later needed back surgery and wasn't able to ride with Butch on his Harley anymore. So he tried Chewy on the bike, and the dog was a natural. Their first ride was a charity event for kids with brain tumors. Then came the memorial rides for veterans. "All over the country," Butch said. "He's been to California twice."

When I met him, Chewy had logged almost a hundred thousand miles on a motorcycle. And still, I wondered how that worked. A dog on a Harley? I hadn't seen them pull into the station; I had met Butch and Chewy in the lobby, and then we'd taken the short walk to the gardens for the interview. I couldn't wait to see Chewy in action. But I also couldn't wait on the question that lingered, the one about cancer. I had to ask, awkward as it was.

"How long do you think he has?"

Butch lowered his eyes and ran his hand through Chewy's fur. "I don't know," he said. Chewy still squinted, as if thinking on the question, too, and I let the moment sit.

Butch at last opened up, said the vet had told him Chewy would live only two to four weeks. But it had been more than six months since the vet's prognosis. "Perhaps God's letting him stay with me a little bit longer to prepare." Another long moment passed. Butch seemed to be on the verge of tears. He looked up. "When he goes, I don't know what I'm going to do."

It was at last time to ride, and I think they were both ready. I was ready to move, too—it's tough interviewing someone while squatting on one knee. Butch cradled Chewy in his arms, walked the few feet to the parking lot and propped him on the Harley. He seat-belted him in, strapped a white helmet on his head and slid a pair of red goggles over his eyes. The goggles were priceless, and I could tell Robert was making sure to get plenty of tight shots. Those apple-red goggles and the silky blue bandana around his neck made him look like one cool cat—or, rather, dog. "Who ya callin' dog face?" read a sticker on his helmet; the helmet was loaded with stickers.

Butch climbed on in front, clad in a leather jacket, jeans, and boots, and there was plenty of room for both. Chewy sat sideways a bit, his head pointed away from Butch's back. That way, he could point his long nose in the wind and breathe the cool air. And slobber.

"And sometimes his slobber will come over," Butch said. "It'll push up and then just come back into my face." He laughed. "Good memories."

He fired up the Harley, and Robert scrambled around to the back where I could tell he had Chewy pictured in the frame, along with a little American flag Butch had mounted to the back of the bike. The flag waved, either from the engine's vibration or afternoon wind. The sky was crystal blue, even that late in the day, but strewn with puffy clouds. I was struck by the perfection of the shot; that is, if the camera saw what I did. The view couldn't have been any better color coordinated: Chewy with red goggles, white helmet, and blue bandana; the little American flag flapping in the foreground; and that big blue-and-puffy sky in the

distance. So much seemed embodied in that one image—patriotism, of course, but also love and loyalty and adventure. And humor. A dog on a motorcycle? Chewy stole the show.

Butch juiced the Harley, and away they went, roaring away from the camera with Robert still focused on them—I hoped he was keeping the shot tight, that he hadn't zoomed out wide; I didn't want viewers to recognize the television station parking lot.

I knew them riding away like that was probably going to be our closing shot, but we were far from finished. We jumped in the car and sped around the corner to Centennial Parkway, propped the camera on the tripod, and grabbed video of Butch and Chewy motoring past us as we had planned, first one way then the other, back and forth. "He's having a good time," Butch said. He wore a headset with a microphone, and I'd clipped my mic to his so we were able to record audio while he was riding. "He's enjoying it. He's sitting straight up, so that's an indicator."

We jumped in the car again and rode alongside them. I drove, Robert rolled, pointing the camera out the passenger-side window; fortunately for us, Centennial was sleepy and without much traffic.

"Chewy's enjoying putting his tongue in the wind," came the crackle of Butch's mic, and I thought also of Chewy's nose in the wind and another sticker I'd seen on his helmet: "Places to go, people to sniff."

He had certainly seen a great many places for a dog. Butch had shown me pictures: Chewy posed by a Route 66 sign somewhere in the dusty midsection of the country. One time, he rode a thousand miles in twenty-four hours, what motorcyclists call an Iron Butt ride—though in Chewy's case, Iron Mutt.

Pictures also showed him hamming it up with pretty girls and pretty girl dogs, Chewy always in those handsome red goggles—except at the gravesides of veterans. There he sat, often captured in profile, sometimes silhouetted, prominent nose pointed forward: proud, respectful, a quiet bond between duty-bound man, now gone, and man's duty-bound friend, forever loyal.

Chewy did not look sick. He looked absolutely delightful seated on the back of the bike, tongue in the wind, wind in his fur. Of all the moments we'd ever captured on camera, the shot of Chewy on the bike with those oh-so-cool apple-red goggles was the one I felt roared to the top, the best shot of all. I suddenly didn't care so much whether viewers recognized Centennial Parkway or the television station parking lot or the well-known azalea gardens. The overriding image would be Chewy; that's what viewers would be sure to remember. A dog on a motorcycle!

We did indeed end the story with that closing shot: Butch and Chewy pulling away, Chewy's red-goggled face filling the screen, the flapping

American flag and distant blue sky streaked with puffy clouds. "I'm comforted knowing this is in God's hands," Butch had told me, his voice soft, and I remembered yet another sticker on Chewy's helmet. I had asked Robert to get a shot of it. It read, "In God we Trust."

Say a prayer for Chewy is the line I scripted for the story's end. It was not a sad ending, not really, not with that precious close-up of goggle-eyed Chewy. Although I supposed the puffy clouds in the distance did suggest uncertainty, albeit mixed with adventure, and hovering over everything was a deep sense of patriotism and, perhaps, an even deeper feeling of faith.

The Harley roared away, and later, over that shot-of-all-shots, I voiced the final line in the audio booth, hoping it would suit, hoping it would live up to the closing video, that perfect shot. Above all, hoping for Chewy.

In God we trust with faith for the road ahead.

POSTSCRIPT

Chewy died on April 3, 2017, almost two years longer than expected. He was fifteen years old.

His death was tough on Butch; I called him again, and his voice was only a whisper. He said what he had before, that day in the gardens. "I don't know what I'm going to do." I expressed my sympathies, and it occurred to me I had also said what I had before, that first time I'd called Butch when he told me Chewy had cancer. I'd expressed my sympathies then, too.

I supposed we had come full circle, and so it only seemed right for the story to do so as well. I told Butch we planned to re-air it with news of Chewy's passing and said I hoped he felt it would be a fitting tribute. He seemed comforted by the thought and told me again how many people Chewy had touched: fellow riders, families of veterans, children with brain tumors. At Chewy's "Celebration of Life" service, motorcyclists had ridden from Florida, Georgia, South Carolina, and Tennessee, all that way to attend a memorial for a dog. People had genuinely loved him, Butch said, people from all over the country, from California to North Carolina. Chewy had lived long enough to surpass a hundred thousand miles.

I watched Chewy's story again the night it re-aired, but even then, seeing him on screen, knowing he had died, I did not feel so terribly sad. In fact, I smiled, even laughed, when I saw him in those red goggles seated on the Harley, looking straight at the camera. One cool . . . dog.

The Harley roared, and Butch began pulling away. Chewy began drifting away. The little American flag flapped on the back of the bike, and the puffy blue sky stretched in the distance.

"So long, Chewy," I wanted to tell him. He was on to his next adventure.

EPILOGUE

THE PLACE I GO

Robert and I have traveled to all of North Carolina's one hundred counties, most of those counties multiple times.

I can't imagine how many miles we've racked up in the dozen years we've been Tar Heel Traveling, but it's probably equal to driving from East Coast to West Coast and back at least a couple of times.

We have aired two thousand Tar Heel Traveler stories, and I remember the first as vividly as the last. Some, of course, are more memorable than others, but none of them blur. Each holds its own little special place in my mind.

"Where do you come up with your ideas?" people ask me, and they're surprised when I tell them it's easy.

Viewers constantly email me. I often get three or four story ideas a day. I print them out, highlight the important information, title them at the top of the page, and file them in folders marked by location. I bet I have five thousand sheets of paper bulging from folders crammed in my file cabinet and stuffed in an old computer bag. That's five thousand stories waiting for me—it might even be ten thousand; I'd hate to count. I'd rather travel. I take it one mile, one story at a time. So little time, so many stories. The stories are everywhere—and not just at my desk.

I write these final thoughts, and you'll never guess where I'm writing them, though I'm sure you've heard of the place; it's a restaurant. Stick with me a moment more, and I'll tell you. I'll also explain why it's relevant.

Most mornings I get up, walk my two dogs—Cavalier King Charles Spaniels—and sneak away to my little place where the staff knows me. I don't even have to order; they're already making my breakfast by the time I step to the counter. I'm a creature of habit; I eat the same item every morning. Drink the same, too: coffee, black.

And here I sit.

It's where I write before I write, my creative writing before my Tar Heel Traveler writing. I work on the book before crafting a script. *A page a day*, I tell myself, which might not sound like much, but I edit as I go, strain over every sentence, click the online thesaurus for just the right word—free Wi-Fi at my little place.

I sit at the same table, and it's not ideal, but that's okay—creature of habit again. The table is by one of the restaurant's big windows. Those big, long windows are all around; there's no escape, but mine, at least, is partly covered by a poster advertising some new food special. The poster partially blocks the sun so I can see my laptop screen, but only if the laptop rests on the table's right side—maybe that's why my left arm is redder than the other.

Curiously, I'm usually the only customer eating inside the restaurant most mornings. Not that the place isn't popular; it is, but people know it more as a lunch and dinner spot. That's okay, too. I enjoy the peace—but could use some more quiet.

The television is on, usually tuned to the Screening Room with the host who fiddles with her hands and talks about the latest movies then shows the trailers. Sometimes they suck me in. Sometimes the restaurant staff does.

The manager is a sweet little lady, originally from Mexico, who has worked at this restaurant for thirty-two years. It's a fast-food restaurant.

"Thirty-two years?" I say. "I didn't know it had even been here that long." She nods and says she could have moved on but likes the food company that owns it. She says she could have moved up in the company but likes the customers, the one-on-one. She speaks with an accent.

"Ever get back to Mexico?" I ask.

"Not much," she says and tells me she's raised a family in Raleigh, three kids, all grown and successful. She steps away to get me my coffee. I don't think she's used to customers asking her such questions, but I'm interested. And impressed. *Thirty-two years in fast food at the very same restaurant . . . She's a story,* I think.

"Gracias," I say. She slides me the cup and smiles.

The young girl in back is still making my breakfast. She stands at a stainless-steel table, which I'm sure in a few hours will become the center of the assembly line, but for now it's just her. Kitchen equipment blocks her face, but I can see her hands, which work quickly and efficiently. She knows what she's doing. And I know who she is. I recognize her arm.

She wears a large tattoo on her right forearm. I'm not much for tattoos, but this one I kind of like. It's intriguing. It's a cross. The crossbeams are thick and colored in; they're dark brown. The image is simple, yet bold.

She soon swings around the blocky equipment to the front, carrying a tray. On it is my breakfast tucked in a see-through plastic wrapper, though clouded with steam. She is such a pretty girl; I think she could be a model. Her eyes are dazzling. I've rarely seen such enthusiasm in someone's eyes.

She's just twenty years old or so, unmarried, but already has a three-year-old son. She goes to school full-time and is attempting to earn some type of medical degree. I'd like to ask more, but it's a fast-food place, and fast food is fast, not meant for conversation. She does tell me she's making all A's, and her eyes, already brilliant, sparkle even more.

There are others: the thirty-ish woman at the register with the beautiful smile who seems rather well-educated. She speaks properly and apparently watches the news. On one of my first visits, she said she recognized me from television, though I think she's kept that little nugget of info between us ever since. She must have deduced this was my quiet place and refrained from telling anyone else. I don't think her coworkers have ever seen the *Tar Heel Traveler*. They're probably too busy working or studying or taking care of children. The thirty-ish woman smiles when I thank her and pay—and even when she hauls out the trash.

An hour drifts by, then two. One cup of coffee has come and gone, and the second one's almost gone. Two is my limit. I could drink more—I love coffee—but too much caffeine can't be healthy.

The coffee is surprisingly good. It is not a place known for coffee. Or even breakfast. It's a place known for Coke, Pepsi, and Mountain Dew and for tacos, bean burritos, and quesadillas. A breakfast quesadilla—bacon bits, scrambled eggs, and cheese wrapped in a tortilla—it's what I get every time at my little place, at the Taco Bell just down the street from the television station.

"Taco Bell?" my friends say. "For breakfast?" They look at me like I'm loco.

It wasn't black coffee I was drinking one Saturday night, but something much stronger when I told them about writing my book at Taco Bell. "There's this whole . . . culture," I said, fumbling for the right word. "The manager from Mexico . . . thirty-two years . . . and the young girl . . . a cross on her arm . . . she could be a model." I'm not sure my friends were getting it; they smirked. "The woman's smile . . . ," I said, but they were soon headed back to the bar.

Maybe it's just me, the reporter in me. I'm sure there are stories at my little breakfast place, all around my little table where I've been writing my stories, my book, this book, the one you're reading now and about to finish. I've been writing these stories to somehow preserve them, and not just the stories but the backstories, too. It's all part of it, just as this place has been part of this book. Maybe you, the reader, should know that as well. There are stories sometimes even in fast-food places where you're the only customer.

Taco Bell and the Tar Heel Traveler—it's an odd combination, but I love surprises in a story—or in this case, a surprise outside the story as I write the story. How about that for irony? I also love an ending with a twist.

The end is near. Two more paragraphs. One last sip. Who knew Taco Bell made such good coffee? I drop the cup in the trash. *I'll be back tomorrow*, I think. *And the day after.* There are so many stories to remember and write about. And so many more left to cover—five thousand and counting. Or is it ten thousand?

Charles Kuralt, that beloved storyteller for CBS News, used to say there are stories everywhere, that all you really have to do is look out the window. His quote comes to mind as I exit the restaurant with those long windows all the way around the building.

And I think, *Sometimes all you really have to do is look* inside *the window.*

INDEX

ABOUT THE AUTHOR

Scott Mason has been a television reporter for thirty-five years and WRAL's Tar Heel Traveler since 2007. His more than one hundred journalism awards include twenty regional Emmys and three National Edward R. Murrow Awards, one of broadcasting's highest honors. He has twice been named North Carolina Television Reporter of the Year. He lives in Raleigh, North Carolina.